# ⤳ *Home By Another Way*

Cowley Publications is a ministry of the brothers of the
Society of Saint John the Evangelist, a monastic order in the
Episcopal Church. Our mission is to provide books and resources
for those seeking spiritual and theological formation. Cowley
Publications is committed to developing a new generation of
writers and teachers who will encourage people to think and pray
in new ways about spirituality, reconciliation, and the future.

·~ BARBARA BROWN TAYLOR

# Home By
# Another Way

A Cowley Publications Book
ROWMAN & LITTLEFIELD PUBLISHERS, INC.
*Lanham · Chicago · New York · Toronto · Plymouth, UK*

A Cowley Publications Book
Published by Rowman & Littlefield Publishers, Inc.
A wholly owned subsidary of The Rowman & Littlefield Publishing Group, Inc.
4501 Forbes Boulevard, Suite 200, Lanham, Maryland 20706
http://www.rowmanlittlefield.com

Estover Road, Plymouth PL6 7PY, United Kingdom

Distributed by National Book Network

British Library Cataloguing in Publication Information Available

Library of Congress Cataloging-in-Publication Data

Taylor, Barbara. Brown.
  Home by another way / Barbara Brown Taylor
    p.   cm.
  ISBN-10: 1-56101-167-3   ISBN-13: 978-1-56101-167-4
  1. Sermons, American—Women authors.   2. Episcopal Church Sermons.
  2. Church year sermons.   4. Anglican Communion Sermons.   I. Title.
  BX5937.T28H65   1999
  252'.6—dc21                                      99-29239

"The Unnatural Truth" first appeared in the *Christian Century*, March 20–27, 1996.
"Lenten Discipline" first appeared as "Settling for Less" in the *Christian Century*,
February 18, 1998. "Life-Giving Fear" first appeared in the *Christian Century*, March
4, 1998. "Three Hands Clapping" was previously published in *The Living Pulpit*. All
are reprinted by permission.

Cover design: Brad Norr Design
Interior design: Wendy Holdman

⊚™ The paper used in this publication meets the minimum requirements of
American National Standard for Information Sciences—Permanence of Paper
for Printed Library Materials, ANSI/NISO Z39.48-1992.
Printed in the United States of America

*For Harry Pritchett*
*who gave me room to grow*

# Contents

# ❧ *Advent and Christmas*

# God's Beloved Thief

MATTHEW 24:37–44

*Keep awake therefore, for you do not know on what day your Lord is coming. But understand this: if the owner of the house had known in what part of the night the thief was coming, he would have stayed awake and would not have let his house be broken into. Therefore you also must be ready, for the Son of Man is coming at an unexpected hour.*

FOR THOSE WHO ARE COUNTING, THE NEXT MILLEN-nium is now thirteen months and one day away. If this is a normal crowd, then some of you could care less while others are genuinely spooked by the idea, and the rest of you are somewhere in between—a little anxious, maybe, but mostly curious about what—if anything—will happen when the world's odometer turns over.

As millennial fervor increases, some of us may try to distance ourselves from it, but we cannot escape altogether. The most basic formulations of the Christian faith all include the expectation of Christ's return. You can hear it when we celebrate communion: "Christ has died. Christ is risen. Christ will come again." You can hear it when we say the creed: "He will come again in glory to judge the living and the dead, and his kingdom will have no end." You can hear it in this morning's gospel lesson, which sets the tone for the new church year: "Keep awake therefore, for you do not know on what day your Lord is coming."

There is no getting away from it, but there may be no reason for losing sleep over it either. Christ has been coming back for so long that plenty of people have given up on him. Before he died, he told his followers he would be right back. Believing him, they did not make long range plans. They put all their energy into preparing for the end. All of Paul's letters were written with the second coming in plain view. Then a decade passed, then another. The people who had actually known Jesus began to die off. Pretty soon the stories about him were being told by people who had known people who had known Jesus. The only reason we have gospels at all is that someone finally worked up the nerve to say, "You know, there aren't all that many eyewitnesses left. We really ought to get this stuff down on paper."

According to anyone's best guess, Matthew's gospel was the second or third one written, about forty years after Jesus' death. Jesus' mother Mary was almost certainly dead by that time, along with the apostles Peter and Paul (both martyred in Rome). Jerusalem had been destroyed by Titus while putting down the Jewish rebellion. The promised land was a province of the Empire. The temple lay in ruins, and the chosen people seemed to have been chosen chiefly to suffer.

All of which is to say that Matthew had a lot of explaining to do. While the main purpose of his gospel was to tell the story of Jesus the Christ, he had to do more than that. He had to tell it to people who were frightened and tired of waiting—people who desperately wanted to know whether Jesus' delay was part of the master plan or whether he was missing in action. Was he really coming back to pull them from the edge of the abyss or were they just going to hang there until their fingers gave out and they fell onto the mounting pile of bodies at the bottom?

Matthew's twenty-fourth chapter is his answer to them, a section of his gospel known as "the little apocalypse," in which he recorded Jesus' sayings about the end time along with a few emphases of his own. Right before we tuned in, he set up the paradox that continues to perplex. First Jesus said, "Truly I tell you, this generation will not pass away until all these things have taken place." Then he said, "But about that day and hour no one knows, neither the angels of heaven, nor the Son, but only the Father."

That was absolutely the best Matthew could do, to put those two contradictory statements right there together where they have continued to chafe against each other for almost two thousand years now. *I'm coming right back, but only God knows when.* Matthew could not resolve the tension without putting words in Jesus' mouth, so what he did instead was to focus on Jesus' own advice about how to live with it: "Keep awake therefore, for you do not know on what day your Lord is coming."

Not knowing has never kept us from guessing, however. Over the years there have been hundreds of wrong guesses about when the Lord would come, some of them based on mathematical readings of the Bible and others on the predictions of self-appointed prophets. On the whole, these forecasts of the end time seem to multiply whenever the present times get grim, and especially when there are two or more zeros in the date.

In the years leading up to the year 1000, religious leaders spoke of the world as *mundus senescit*, "a world grown old and senile, ripe for well-deserved oblivion."[1] Many people believed the day of judgment would come exactly one thousand years after Jesus' birth, and their fears were confirmed by what they saw going on around them.

In the tenth century, Europe was under attack, with ferocious Slavs invading from the east while militant Muslims swarmed up from the south. Meanwhile, the air was thick with pollution from countless wood fires and sewage ran in the streets. People saw meteors in the sky and volcanoes on earth. When Pope Sylvester stood motionless in front of the altar at the conclusion of the mass on New Year's Eve 999, no one breathed as the church bell began to ring midnight. *One, two, three*—now is the time to repent you of your sins—*four, five, six*—any second now, half of us may be gone—*seven, eight, nine*—hold tight to your children's hands; are all of them baptized?—*ten, eleven, twelve*—look, the Pope is still there with his hands in the air—look, so are we, alleluia! God has seen fit to spare our lives! Thanks be to God!

According to Matthew, the funniest thing about this scenario is that people believe the Christ will come back when everyone is wide awake and ready. They think he uses the same daytimer they do, with all the same holidays and the same number of sheets. For Matthew, this is about as laughable as believing that a thief will ring you up first to see when might be a good time for him to break into your house. Would Monday be all right? Or would Thursday work better for you?

It will never happen, anymore than Jesus will come back on a published schedule, surrounded by the press. Instead he will come back like a thief in the night, with a wool cap pulled down low on his head and socks on his feet so that you do not even know he is there until you wake up to the sound of someone breathing over you in your bed.

If this has ever really happened to you—or even if you have ever come home to find your back door standing wide open and your television set gone—then you know what a troubling image of God this is. To have your home robbed is to feel broken into at some very deep level of your being. The idea of some stranger going through your drawers, handling your things, looking at the pictures on your bureau—knowing where your children sleep and what kinds of toys they take to bed with them—violates one of our most precious illusions: that our homes are our safe places, our private places, where we can protect ourselves from the world and all its threats.

According to Matthew, this intruder is a thief and not a murderer, but he is still a scary character. He is someone with no respect for other people's boundaries. He sees the home security sign in the front yard as a helpful clue to the kind of system he must dismantle. He sees a door full of deadbolts as an invitation to come in by the bathroom window instead. If he is really good at what he does, then there is no way to keep him out. All he has to do is watch you and you will show him the way in.

The question is, what is he after? If he is who Matthew says he is, then he is not interested in your jewelry or your television set. He is interested in you, although apparently not in the daytime you—the one most people see while you are out doing whatever it is you do in the world, pulled together well enough so that you pass for normal—making it to your lunch meeting on time, answering the telephone, opening the mail, stopping by the dry cleaners on the way home. Whatever else is going on inside of you, it is usually possible to manage it during the daylight hours, if only because everyone around you seems to be managing too.

Then you get home and the children are needy, or the cat is hungry, or the message machine is blinking so fast you cannot count the lights. Once you have dealt with them all, it is dark. The sink is full of dishes. The news is on. Tonight is the night you were going to balance the checkbook. When do people actually *live* their lives, given all the other things they have to do? The evening passes the way so many do. It is over before you know it and you are the last one awake. You check the doors and the windows before you head off to bed. You leave the kitchen light on. The dog sighs as you pass her on your way up the stairs. There is not another sound in the house.

Now is when you should listen out for that thief, because now is when he is interested in you—when you think no one is watching, when you think you are alone. If you were expecting him he would not come, but since you are not expecting anything save a few uneventful hours in bed, now is an excellent time for him to slip past your defenses, to disarm your security system and enter your safe space.

Why would a compassionate Lord do a thing like that? You know why. Because you are so well protected the rest of the time. Because it is the only time when your guard is down. After years of steady practice, you have learned how to keep almost everyone and everything at a safe distance from you while you are awake, but any good thief knows that even you have to sleep. That is why he waits until way after dark. That is why he comes when you least expect him—because he knows how badly you need to be broken into, and how hard you will resist.

Like any other thief, this one is after your valuables, but unlike any other, this one knows what they really are: not your silver and your stereo but your heart, your soul, your mind. Those are the treasures this thief's own heart is set on, at no small risk to his life. Who knows what you have under that pillow, or how loud you can yell? Who knows what lengths you will go to, to protect yourself?

It would be a lot safer for *him* to send you a letter by registered mail, announcing that your prayers have been answered. Next Thursday at six, the kingdom will come. All will be revealed. Since you will have no further use for anything on earth, you are hereby relieved of protecting it. You are free. You may let go—of your carefully guarded stuff, your carefully guarded self, your carefully guarded list of things to do. Next Thursday at six none of that will matter anymore. Everything good will be changed into light, and everything else into fire. P.S.: Jesus will come by for you at five.

Can you guess what your reaction to that might be? But I have season tickets to the symphony! But my daughter is about to have a baby! But I haven't finished my degree! But I thought I would have more time! Can't I have a little more time? There are some people I need to say good-bye to. There are a few things I need to straighten out first. At least give me time to clean out my refrigerator.

"But understand this: if the owner of the house had known in what part of the night the thief was coming, he would have stayed awake and would not have let his house be broken into." That is why God does not send registered mail. That is why Jesus will come back like a thief in the night: so that we do not have time to lock him out. As long as we are successful at that, we will never know what a peculiar thief this really is, who comes not to take but to give.

If we could ever once handle our fear of his intrusion—if we could ever once let him in to do his work—then we might find him emptying his pockets instead of filling them, giving us so much more than the poor little piles we have spent our lives protecting. The threat is not outside the door. It is inside us: in our misplaced fears, our misguided defenses.

Keep awake, therefore—not to keep the intruder out but to let him in. He may be a thief, but he is God's beloved thief, who has come to set us free.

### Notes

1. Richard Erdoes, "Living on the Brink of Apocalypse," *Parabola* (Spring 1998), 46.

# Wherever the Way May Lead

*The beginning of the good news of Jesus Christ, the Son of God.
As it is written in the prophet Isaiah, "See, I am sending my
messenger ahead of you, who will prepare your way."*

Mark's gospel does not begin with angels whispering in Mary's ear. There are no shepherds keeping watch over their flocks by night, no wise men from the east following a star, no big-eyed animals standing around a straw-stuffed manger. Mark either did not know about those things or else he did not care about them. For him, the good news of Jesus Christ begins in the wilderness of Judea with an old-timey prophet named John, the first real prophet to turn up in Israel in three hundred years.

If Mark's gospel were a movie, here is how it would begin. First, a long pan shot of the desert east of Jerusalem: row upon row of buckskin-colored hills with nothing on them but rock and sand and silence. In the distance, a Bedouin shepherd dressed in black leads his sheep up one of the hills, and as they disappear over the other side of it the title appears on the screen, just the way we heard it a moment ago: "The beginning of the good news of Jesus Christ, the Son of God." It is a long title, but there is plenty of room for it, with all that desert.

Then you hear a man's voiceover as the camera continues to scan the hills. "As it is written in the prophet Isaiah," the voice says. "'See, I am sending my messenger ahead of you, who will prepare your way,'" it says, and people appear on the screen, walking toward something you cannot see. As you watch, they come to the edge of a big crowd and push into it, straining for a better view of what is going on up front.

"'The voice of one crying out in the wilderness,'" the voice goes on. "'Prepare the way of the Lord, make his paths straight.'" And just then the camera breaks through the crowd to show you the strange-looking man at the center of the commotion. He is standing knee-deep in the Jordan River, with a soaking wet person shivering beside him. He does not look like anyone else around him. As different as they are from one another, the others at least look like they come from the same century, while the man they have come to see looks like a cave man.

He is dressed in camel's hair with a leather belt, the exact same outfit Elijah wore eight hundred years before him. His hair and his beard look like they have never been cut and he is skinny as a cactus. Surely this is a statement of some kind. Those of us watching the movie may not be able to interpret it very well, but those standing around him certainly could. The man was a messenger—predicted by Isaiah, dressed like Elijah, sent by God—a prophet in the classic mold.

Maybe that is why people flocked to him. I cannot figure it out. Everything I know about him makes me think I would have gone out of my way *not* to see him. He sounds too much like those street evangelists who wave their Bibles at you and tell you that you are going straight to hell if you do not repent right now (and of course they are the only ones who know how you are supposed to do that and whether or not you have passed the test). Only there was one big difference between them and John.

Self-appointed prophets tend to plant themselves right in your way so you have to cross to the other side of the street to avoid them. They get in your face and dare you to ignore them, whereas John planted himself in the middle of nowhere. He set up shop in the wilderness, and anyone who wanted to hear what he had to say had to go to a lot of trouble to get there, borrowing the neighbor's donkey or setting off on foot with enough water for the journey, which led down lonely trails infested with bandits.

You have to wonder why someone would do a thing like that, especially someone from Jerusalem, which was where the temple was, and the rabbis, and all the accumulated wisdom of the religious establishment. If someone wanted to hear from God, why not stay right there, maybe attend some extra services or make an appointment with one of the chief priests? Anyone who would turn away from all that and set off for the wilderness was looking for something else, something the temple could not or would not supply.

John had it, apparently. He was scary, all right. He was uncivilized. He was from another planet, but he spoke about the one who was coming as if he were repeating what God was saying to him right that moment, one sentence at a time. He did not have many details. He did not know the name of the one who was coming, for instance, or what *he* looked like, but he knew that the old world was about to end and a new world was spinning toward him, carried in the arms of God's chosen one.

It was a world that would be built out of new materials, not the rearranged stones of the old religion. The Holy Spirit had gotten all but covered up in Jerusalem, with pretend piety and temple taxes and priestly hocus-pocus. The flame was all but snuffed out under the weight of all that foppery, so God moved it—out into the wilderness, where the air was sharp and clean, out under the stars where it was fanned by the most socially unacceptable character anyone could imagine. Dressed in animal hair with a piece of tanned hide around his waist, his breath heavy with locusts and wild honey, John proclaimed that Someone was coming, someone so spectacular that it was not enough simply to hang around waiting for him to arrive. It was time to get ready, to prepare the way, so that when he came he could walk a straight path right to their doors.

That was the good news John was the beginning of. He was the messenger, and the message lit him up like a bonfire in the wilderness. People were drawn to him, apparently, not only because of who he was and what he said but also because of what he offered them—a chance to come clean, to stop pretending they were someone else and start over again, by allowing him to wash them off. The bath was his own idea. There were not any rules about how it was supposed to be done. The rabbis had not okayed it. It was just something John offered those who came to him—even women, who were not allowed in the inner precincts of the temple—even well-known sinners, who would not have dreamed of trying to get inside at all. John's baptism bypassed the temple and all its rites. Setting up shop in the wilderness, he proclaimed his freedom from so-called civilization, with all its rules and requirements. He called people to wake up, to turn around, so that they would not miss the new thing God was doing right before their eyes.

The gospel always begins with a messenger, whether it is an angel whispering in Mary's ear or a parent telling a child a story or a skinny prophet standing knee-deep in a river. What strikes me about this messenger—this John the Baptist one—is that he was nowhere near a church, and those who insisted on staying inside the church never heard his message. Only those who were willing to enter the wilderness got to taste his freedom, and many of them were still there when the spectacular Someone arrived, far from the civilized center of town.

I reckon every one of us has some idea where our own wilderness lies, as well as a long list of all the good reasons why we should not go there. We are comfortable here, after all. We know the ropes and we know we will be fed. Why should we hunt God anywhere else? I cannot imagine, unless it is that voice crying out in the wilderness, the one you cannot quite make out from here. If we only listen for God in church, we will miss half of the message. The good news is always beginning somewhere in the world, for those with ears to hear and hearts to go wherever the way may lead.

# Singing Ahead of Time

—

LUKE 1:39–56

*And Mary said, "My soul magnifies the Lord, and my spirit rejoices in God my Savior, for he has looked with favor on the lowliness of his servant. Surely, from now on all generations will call me blessed; for the Mighty One has done great things for me, and holy is his name."*

ONE LIABILITY OF HAVING HEARD THE CHRISTMAS story over and over again is that we all know how it turns out. There is no way to recapture the initial shock of the news: that God is coming in the flesh to show us what real life looks like.

For the past couple of weeks, John the Baptist has been the messenger of that news. If you have been here, or have kept up with the lessons at home, then you know that the news has not been all that good. There has been a lot of talk about axes, pitchforks, and unquenchable fires. There has been the suggestion that we are snakes in the grass—vipers, to be exact—who only seek God when our own snake pits are on fire. So it is a real relief this morning to hear from a different messenger—not John the Baptist but Mary the Prophet, who will also turn out to be Mary the mother of Jesus, but not yet. Today she is still a maiden, chosen by God to bear a message before she ever bears a child.

Her cousin Elizabeth is the first one to hear what Mary has to say, maybe because Elizabeth is the first one willing to listen. She too is pregnant, Luke says—about six months further along than Mary, and much, much older—so old, in fact, that her impending motherhood is as much a miracle as Mary's. So she and Mary have a lot in common. The obvious difference is that, in Elizabeth's case, there is a biological father hanging around— Zechariah by name, a priest in the order of Abijah who has not said a word in months.

We almost never hear his story in church, which is too bad, since he and Mary have something in common too. According to Luke, they have both been visited by the angel Gabriel, who went to tell Zechariah about his and Elizabeth's baby-to-be before he ever went to tell Mary about hers. Unfortunately, Zechariah's annunciation did not go as well as Mary's did. When the angel told Zechariah that Elizabeth would bear a son whose name would be John, Zechariah said, "How will I know that this is so? For I am an old man, and my wife is getting on in years." For this apparent impertinence, the angel zipped Zechariah's lips, making him mute until the day he heard his son cry out for the first time.

Six months later, when Gabriel told Mary that *she* would bear a son, she said more or less the same thing. "How can this be, since I am a virgin?" But for some reason the angel went easier on her. He told her that the Holy Spirit would come upon her, that the power of the Most High would overshadow her, and instead of asking any more questions, she said, "Here am I, the servant of the Lord; let it be with me according to your word."

So when she goes to visit Elizabeth and Zechariah, Mary can still speak, while all he can do is wave. Poor Zechariah. It is all women's voices in the house that day. First Mary, greeting her cousin Elizabeth, and then Elizabeth, who does not *say* what she says next, the way we make it sound in church, but who exclaims with a loud cry, "Blessed are you among women, and blessed is the fruit of your womb." Why is Elizabeth talking so loudly? Because she is excited that Mary has come to see her. Because her own baby has jumped for joy inside of her. Because there is new life popping out all over and she is so glad her young cousin has the good sense to believe that what is happening to her is not an accident, nor an illusion, nor a freak of nature, but a wedding gift from God.

After Elizabeth lets loose it is Mary's turn again. You would think that at a time like this she would settle down with Elizabeth and compare notes on their appetites, their mood swings, their backaches and swelling feet. Elizabeth was ahead of Mary, after all. She could have warned her about some things and given her some others to look forward to, but instead of the elder woman sharing her wisdom with the younger, it is the younger who enlightens the elder, launching into a prophecy that we repeat to this day.

"My soul magnifies the Lord," Mary sings right there in Elizabeth's living room, "and my spirit rejoices in God my Savior." Elizabeth and Zechariah are the first to hear her song, but it is not just for them. It is also for her, Mary, and for the Mighty One who has done great things for her. It is for Gabriel, who first gave her the good news, and for all who will benefit from it—for the proud and powerful who will be relieved of their swelled heads, for the hungry who will be filled with good things, for the rich who will be sent away empty so that they have room in them for more than money can buy. Her song is for Abraham, Isaac, and Jacob—for Sarah, Rebecca, Leah, and Rachel—for every son and daughter of Israel who thought God had forgotten the promise to be with them forever, to love them forever, to give them fresh and endless life.

It was all happening inside of Mary, and she was so sure of it that she was singing about it ahead of time—not in the future tense but in the past, as if the promise had already come true. Prophets almost never get their verb tenses straight, because part of their gift is being able to see the world as God sees it—not divided into things that are already over and things that have not happened yet, but as an eternally unfolding mystery that surprises everyone—maybe even God.

In this divine dance we are all dancing, God may lead but it is entirely up to us whether we will follow. Just because God sends an angel to invite one girl onto the dance floor is no guarantee she will say yes. Just because God sends a prophet to tell us how life on earth can be more like life in heaven does not mean any of us will quit our day jobs to make it so. God acts. Then it is our turn. God responds to us. Then it is our turn again.

The only thing that is absolutely sure in this scenario is that we have a partner who is with us and for us and who wants us to have life. Mary's trust in that fact is really all she has. What she does not have is a sonogram, or a husband, or an affidavit from the Holy Spirit that says, "The child really is mine. Now leave the poor girl alone." All she has is her unreasonable willingness to believe that the God who has chosen her will be part of whatever happens next—and that, apparently, is enough to make her burst into song. She does not wait to see how things will turn out first. She sings ahead of time, and all the angels with her.

If there are any big changes going on with you right now—if something is under way you cannot predict the end of, and your stomach is rolling with your own version of morning sickness—then you might try following Mary's lead. Who knows? Maybe the Holy Spirit has come upon you. Maybe that shadow hanging over you is the power of the Most High.

While it would certainly be nice to have some details about how it will all turn out, that is not really necessary, is it? You know how God has acted in the past, and you know what happens when people say, "Yes, thanks, I'd love to dance." Given all of that, I don't know why you would wait to get excited until you knew for sure how it all turned out.

You seem to me like just the kind of people who would bump into each other getting out on the dance floor before the band leader ever showed up. You seem to me like just the kind of people who would start singing ahead of time.

May your souls magnify the Lord, and your spirits rejoice in God your Savior. For he has looked with favor on you, and all generations will call you blessed. For the Mighty One has done great things for you, and holy is his name.

# Past Perfection

CHRISTMAS EVE
LUKE 2:1–20

*While they were there, the time came for her to deliver her child. And she gave birth to her firstborn son and wrapped him in bands of cloth, and laid him in a manger, because there was no place for them in the inn.*

C AN YOU FEEL IT? THE HUM IN THE AIR TONIGHT, as all our preparations come to an end and the celebration begins. I don't think it is just us, either. I think all of creation is humming tonight, when the membrane between heaven and earth is so thin you can almost see through it. Tonight is the night we measure all time against. Everything that happened yesterday is *before* Christ and everything that happens tomorrow is *after* him. Tonight we are living in the eternal *now* of God's coming among us. His name is Emmanuel—the God who is with us— who is made out of the same stuff we are and who is made out of the same stuff God is and who will not let either of us go.

That is the main thing we are waiting for tonight—for that baby's cry. But that is not the only thing, because most of us are waiting for more than one thing and they are not all the same. For instance, I believe someone here is waiting to find out what is inside that large flat box propped against the wall by the Christmas tree. And someone else is looking forward to waking up in a house in which all the beds are full once again, with children and grandchildren who have come home for the holidays. Some of you have a new baby at your house, which means you are waiting for the first Christmas morning when you wake up in your own live nativity scene.

I know others of you for whom this is a hard time of the year. There is that empty chair to deal with, that stocking that stays folded in the box. All the rituals that were designed for two or more are now up to you alone and it is like the sound of one hand clapping. Christmas is the season when you wait to see if the hurt has let up any since this time last year—and you want it to, so you can get on with your life—and you don't want it to, because that might mean you have stopped caring. Meanwhile, the memories rise up to meet you, swamping you with a melancholy so sweet you can almost taste it in the back of your throat.

For good or ill, every Christmas Eve functions like a kind of time machine for us, taking us back to every other Christmas Eve we have spent on this earth. For some, it is a reminder of the way life used to be, back when we were on the front row of the holiday show and not the stage managers of it. Christmas is the smell of pine boughs and oranges stuck with cloves, the taste of roast turkey and peppermint. It is mom and dad sitting around in their bathrobes sipping coffee while the kids chase the new puppy through a sea of wrapping paper.

For others, this night is a reminder of the way life should have been but never was—those who have looked all their lives through other people's windows at such scenes of domestic bliss, but always as a peeping torn and never as an insider. Everyone is supposed to go home for Christmas, right? Only where is that, exactly? Some of us know and some of us are still trying to find out, but tonight the answer is, *right here.* This is our home to-night, and we are all inside. This is our Bethlehem, where we have hauled the hopes and fears of all our years to lay them in front of a manger.

No wonder the place is humming! It is full of all our Christmas dreams and memories, all our best wishes for ourselves and others, including our ideas about what our lives should be like once God has been born into them. If you are not sure what your ideas are, you can generally find some clues by looking at the Christmas cards you sent this year. Or if you did not send any, then look at the ones you received that you like. What kinds of images are on them? What kinds of words? Unless you or your friends have really strange taste, chances are that "peace," "joy," and "love" are on a lot of them, along with pictures that embody those words. And if you are lucky, you actually got to walk around in some of those pictures this season. You got to experience some peace, some joy, some love—maybe enough to wonder why you do not walk around in them more often.

However different our Christmases have been, one longing most people have in common this time of year is the longing for a calmer, purer, more centered life, and the way most people talk about that life usually has a lot of "up" words in it—as in "rising above anxiety," "keeping our heads above water," or "lifting our eyes up unto the hills," as if belonging to God were a matter of being transported to God's presence for as long as possible, to a place like this one where everything is beautiful, and focused, and right. Just like a Christmas card!

But do you know what? Even the pictures on our Christmas cards are only moments in time. If we could see past the edges, we would probably see some pretty familiar sights. I have one card of a cozy little cabin snuggled in some snowy woods, with one set of tire tracks running up to the door—but I bet the lot next door has been clear-cut to make way for a subdivision, and that there is at least one rusted-out refrigerator in the woods.

I hope I am not ruining your Christmas. What I mean is, even the very best pictures of Emmanuel and his family, the ones where the artist has really focused in on the softness of the baby's skin, the warm bodies of the animals standing around him heating the air with their breath—some of whom might even have licked him if Joseph and Mary had not been standing in the way, bending over him as if they were protecting God himself—even those pictures do not tell the whole story.

You know it by heart—how the whole town was clogged with travelers, none of whom was there by choice. The emperor wanted them all counted and taxed and he could have cared less where they slept. That was their problem, not his. Still, you have to wonder what happened to Joseph's family. If Bethlehem was his hometown, then why didn't his own people take him in? I don't know, but they didn't. Joseph and Mary got a stall instead of a room, which was not as bad as we sometimes make it out to be, but still, not an ideal situation. With luck, they also got a pitchfork and a wheelbarrow. We know they got a feed trough, because that was where they laid their treasure, and that is when the picture was taken—right then, while the star was still overhead and the angels were still singing in the rafters.

But twenty minutes later, what? The hole in the heavens had closed up and the only music came from the bar at the inn. One of the cows stepped on a chicken and the resulting racket made the baby cry. As she leaned over to pick him up, Mary started crying too and when Joseph tried to comfort her she told him she wanted her mother. If she had just married a nice boy from Nazareth, she said, she would be back home where she belonged instead of competing with sheep for a place to sleep.

Then she said she was sorry and Joseph said not to think

another thing about it. He meant it, too. They both hurt all over and there was nothing to eat and it was cold as the dickens, but you know what? God was still there, right in the middle of the picture. Peace was there, and joy, and love—not only in the best of times but also and especially in the worst of times—because during those times there could be no mistake about who was responsible.

It was God-With-Us. Not the God-Up-There somewhere who answers our prayers by lifting us out of our lives, but the God who comes to us in the midst of them—however far from home we are, however less than ideal our circumstances, however much or little our lives reflect the Christmas cards we send. That is where God is born, just there, in any cradle we will offer him, on any pile of straw we will pat together with our hands.

Any of us who have prayed to be transported into God's presence this Christmas will get our wish—only not, perhaps, in the way we had thought. None of heaven's escalators are going up tonight. Everybody up there is coming down tonight, right here, right into our own Bethlehem, bringing us the God who has decided to make his home in our arms.

## *Epiphany*

# Home by Another Way

MATTHEW 2:1–12

*In the time of King Herod, after Jesus was born in Bethlehem
of Judea, wise men from the East came to Jerusalem, asking,
"Where is the child who has been born king of the Jews? For we
observed his star at its rising, and have come to pay him homage."*

THE STORY OF THE MAGI RANKS RIGHT UP THERE
with the Christmas and Easter stories in terms of snaring
the human imagination. Poets as distinct as William Butler Yeats
and William Carlos Williams have wrapped words around the
visit of the wise men. Longfellow even gave them names: Melchior,
Caspar, and Balthasar. Hundreds of artists have painted the
scene, including Botticelli and Fra Angelico. Have you ever seen
Ghirlandaio's "Adoration," painted in 1487? In it, the eldest magus
kneels before the Christ child, who coyly lifts his own loincloth
to let the old man admire his full humanity.

In more recent years, Garrison Keillor has told the story on
National Public Radio's "Prairie Home Companion," and James
Taylor has written a lilting song from which the title of this sermon comes. So much has been made of this story about which
we know so little. They were not kings, of course, and there were
not three of them, at least not according to Matthew. We do not

know who they were, where they came from, or how many of them there were. We do not know how long it took them to get to Bethlehem or how old Jesus was by the time they got there. We are not even sure about that famous star.

It is not that the facts don't matter. It is just that they don't matter as much as the stories do, and stories can be true whether they happen or not. You do not have to do archaeology to find out if they are genuine, or spend years in the library combing ancient texts. There is another way home. You just listen to the story. You let it come to life inside of you, and then you decide on the basis of your own tears or laughter whether the story is true. If you are in any doubt, it is always a good idea to watch other people who have listened to the story—just pay attention to how the story affects them over time. Does it make them more or less human? Does it open them up or shut them down? Does it increase their capacity for joy?

Once upon a time there were three—yes, three—very wise men who were all sitting in their own countries minding their own business when a bright star lodged in the right eye of each one of them. It was so bright that none of them could tell whether it was burning in the sky or in their own imaginations, but they were so wise they knew it did not matter all that much. The point was, something beyond them was calling them, and it was a tug they had been waiting for all their lives.

Each in his own country had tried books, tried magic, tried astrology and reflexology. One had spent his entire fortune learning how to read and write runes. Another lived on nothing but dried herbs boiled in water. The third could walk on hot coals but it did nothing for him beyond the great sense of relief he felt at the end.

They were all glad for a reason to get out of town—because that was clearly where the star was calling them, out—away from everything they knew how to manage and survive, out from under the reputations they had built for themselves, the high expectations, the disappointing returns. And so they set out, one by one, each believing that he was the only one with a star in his eye until they all ran into one another on the road to Jerusalem.

From a distance, each thought the other to be a mirage at first, a twinkling reflection made out of vapor and heat. But as they drew near to one another they saw the star they had in common and it was like a tattoo, or a secret handshake, that made them brothers before they spoke. They were unanimous that the star was leading them to Jerusalem, which made perfect sense, since they had every reason to believe they were on their way to meet a king.

They had no trouble gaining entrance to the palace. They looked rich, and that was enough to get them a royal audience, only the king they met was something of a disappointment. He was old and fat and he had terrible breath. His skin was yellow, as if his bile had gotten the best of him, and the guards on either side of him shook so that their spears jingled against their shields. Without even conferring with one another, the wise men knew he was not the one, so they asked him if he knew of any other kings in the general area.

He had been picking at his fingernails until then, but their question seemed to get his attention in a big way. He looked right at them for the first time, and when he saw the stars in their eyes, his own eyes grew perfectly round, like the eyes of a snake. Asking the wise men if they would please excuse him for a moment, the king stepped into his chapel to confer with his clergy, who whipped out their concordances and told him what he wanted to know. Yes, there was a little something in the book of Micah about a new ruler for Israel, but nothing to get excited about. It had been there a long time. It seemed unlikely, but sure, why not?

Send the wise men to Bethlehem to do the reconnaissance work and save a little bit on the national security budget.

So that was what the king did. He gargled, combed his hair, and went back to tell the wise men they should go to Bethlehem at once—with his blessing—on the condition that they come back and tell him who his successor was so he could send flowers. His breath smelled like Pine-Sol and the wise men left feeling queasy, but once they were back out in the night air they could see the star clearly again and followed it right to the doorway of a one-room house in Bethlehem.

It was a perfectly nice place, modest but well built. It just was not the kind of place they had expected to find a king. A dog was sniffing the woodpile under the eaves in hopes of a mouse. Someone was practicing the lute next door, going over the same phrase again and again. The smell of dinner was still in the air— wheat cakes cooked on a griddle greased with sheep's fat, lentils with lots of garlic and rice. If they had chosen the place them- selves they might never have knocked, but the star had chosen it, so they did, and when the door opened the couple inside almost died of fright.

Not that the wise men noticed. With their arms full of gifts, they crowded into the small space, bumping their turbans on the rafters and snagging their robes on the rough furniture. All they could see was the baby, who was *not* afraid, and whose right eye shone with the same star they had seen before they ever left home. It was he, then, whoever he was. They did not have a clue, but they knew what to do. They got on their knees and worshiped him. Then they gave him the things they had brought him—all the wrong things, they could see now, things he had no use for. They should have brought goat's milk, a warm blanket, something shiny to hang above his crib, only how could they have guessed?

The child's parents were gracious. They thanked the foreigners for their gifts and held them up for the baby to see. Then, to the wise men's complete alarm, the child's mother picked him up and handed him around, so that each one of them held that damp, soft, living weight in his arms. Then she took him back and nursed him until they all fell asleep where they sat.

In the morning, the wise men could not find their stars anywhere. They looked in all the corners and under the chairs. The baby's mother even shook out his blankets but after an initial panic the wise men said never mind, they did not need them anymore. They had found what they were looking for and they could not lose that. As much as they hated to, they guessed they had better be on their way.

No, they would not be going back through Jerusalem, they said. All three of them had had a dream that said steer clear of Jerusalem, as if they needed to be told. If anyone in Jerusalem knew anything at all they would be here instead of there. Besides, none of their old maps worked anymore. They would find a new way home. So the wise men picked up their packs, which were lighter than before, and then they lined up in front of the baby to thank him for the gifts he had given them. "What in the world are you talking about?" the baby's mother laughed, and they told her so she could tell him later.

"For this home and the love here," said the first wise man, who could not remember how to say it in runes.

"For baby flesh," said the second wise man, who had no interest in living on herbs anymore.

"For a really great story," said the third wise man, who thought telling it might do a lot more for him than walking on coals.

Then the wise men trooped outside, stretched, kissed the baby good-bye, and went home by another way.

# The River of Life

THE BAPTISM OF CHRIST

MARK 1:7–11

*In those days Jesus came from Nazareth of Galilee and was baptized by John in the Jordan. And just as he was coming up out of the water, he saw the heavens torn apart and the Spirit descending like a dove on him. And a voice came from heaven, "You are my Son, the Beloved; with you I am well pleased."*

I JUST FINISHED A BOOK CALLED *THE PATRON SAINT of Liars* by a young author named Ann Patchett. It is the story of Rose Clinton and her daughter Cecilia, who live at Saint Elizabeth's Home for Unwed Mothers in Habit, Kentucky. Rose is the cook and Cecilia is the darling of the place, petted and mothered by all the young women who will give their own babies up for adoption. One May day when she is fifteen years old, Cecilia meets one of the new girls who has come to Saint Elizabeth's. Her name is Lorraine. She is skinny, with a head of red curls, and she is about to have a nervous breakdown while she waits to be interviewed by Mother Corinne, the nun in charge. Cecilia decides to help her out by giving her some advice.

"The guy who got you pregnant," she tells Lorraine. "Don't say he's dead. Everybody does that. It makes Mother Corinne crazy."

Lorraine sits on her hands and is quiet for a minute. "I was going to say that," she says.

"See?"

"So what do I tell her?"

"I don't know," Cecilia says. "Tell her the truth. Or tell her you don't remember."

"What did you tell her?" Lorraine asks and Cecilia is speechless. "I sat there, absolutely frozen," she wrote later. "I felt like I had just been mistaken for some escaped mass murderer. I felt like I was going to be sick, but that would only have proved her assumption. No one had ever, ever mistaken me for one of them, not even as a joke. The lobby felt small and airless. I thought I was going to pass out."

It was because she had been mistaken for one of *them*—one of the weak people whose bad decisions had derailed their lives, who had done something so shameful that their own families had packed them off to live with strangers until the evidence could be put up for adoption. In theological terms, Cecilia thought she was going to pass out because she had been mistaken for a sinner, when she had done absolutely nothing wrong.

It was not that she disliked sinners. She had grown up with them. She was friendly and helpful and gave them good advice. She just never expected to be mistaken for one of them, because in her own mind she was of another order of being. She was a virgin, and she thought it was something anyone could see.

An opposite kind of thing happened the day that Jesus showed up at the Jordan to be baptized by John. The place was teeming with sinners—faulty, sorry, guilty human beings—who hoped against hope that John could clean them up and turn their lives around. If you have ever read the arrest record in the newspaper, then you know the kinds of things most of them were guilty of—drunk driving, bad checks, petty larceny, assault. Some were notorious sinners, and some were there for crimes of the heart known only to themselves, but none of them had illusions of their own innocence. They had come to be cleaned. They knew they were not clean.

Then Jesus showed up and got in line with them. No one knew anything about him yet. In Mark's gospel, there are no accounts of Jesus' birth. His life begins with his baptism, so the crowds did not part when he appeared. He simply took his place in line and waited his turn, but later, after the heavens were torn apart and the voice from heaven made clear who he was, there was a *lot* of controversy. What was he doing in that crowd of sinners, looking and acting like one of them? What did he have to be sorry about, and why was God's Beloved submitting himself to a scruffy character like John?

The Christian church has never been comfortable with the baptism of Jesus. Compare the accounts of it in each of the four gospels and you cannot miss the un-ease of the authors. Matthew elaborates on Mark's story by adding that John tried to talk Jesus out of being baptized, and Luke will not even come out and say it was John who did it. The fourth gospel is the most ticklish of all. In it, John bears witness that he saw the Spirit descend like a dove upon Jesus, but he does not mention anything about a baptism at all. Scholars say all this embarrassment is our surest proof Jesus really was baptized by John, because when someone tells you something that it is not in his best interest for you to know, then you can be reasonably sure he is telling you the truth.

If Jesus had listened to his public relations people, he would have been more like Cecilia wanted to be—a friend to sinners, a kind and loving helper, but never mistaken for one of them. His handlers would never, ever have allowed him to be baptized. He could have stood on shore and offered words of encouragement to those going into the water, yes. He could have held out his hand to those who struggled out of the river in their heavy wet clothes, yes, but he could not under any circumstances have gone into the water himself, unless it was to tap John on the shoulder and say, "Hey, you go rest. I'll take over for a while."

Even if he were innocent, even if his intentions were nothing but good, it was ruinous to his reputation. Who was going to believe that he was there just because he cared about those people and refused to separate himself from them? Gossip being what it was, who was not going to think that he had just a few teeny-weeny things to get off his conscience before he went into public ministry?

You see the problem. We spend a lot of time in the Christian church talking about God's love for sinners, but we sure do go to a lot of trouble not to be mistaken for one of them. Guilt by association and all that. Only Jesus—our leader and our Lord—did not seem too concerned about that. In him, God's being-with-us included God's being in the river with us, in the flesh with us, in the sorrow of repentance and the joy of new life with us. So what if he did not have anything of his own to be sorry about?

When we confess our sins here, we do not simply confess our own personal sins. We kneel and talk to God about the sins of all humankind—all the things we, as a people, have done and failed to do, all the ways we have fled from the love of God because we are afraid to be seen, known, and changed. And when we celebrate the gift of new life here, we do not do it simply for ourselves. We say our alleluias on behalf of all those who have discovered hope in the midst of despair, light in the midst of darkness, life in the midst of death. Nothing we do here is a private matter between us and God. Like Jesus in the river, this is something we do in union—in communion—with all humankind.

"Will you seek and serve Christ in all persons, loving your neighbor as yourself?" That is one of the questions we will answer together in a moment, one of five that form the heart of our faith. "Will you strive for justice and peace among all people, and respect the dignity of every human being?"

Whenever we welcome new members into the household of God, we begin with this baptismal covenant. We say it with them, so we all remember what is expected of us: to believe in God, Father, Son, and Holy Spirit; to take our places at God's table and grow strong on God's food; never to give up on ourselves, but always—in what we say and what we do—to proclaim the good news that God has come among us in the flesh. Then we invite the newcomers to step into the river with Jesus, so that their beings are wrapped up with all other human beings: the well ones and the hurt ones, the brave ones and the weak ones, the successful ones and the ones who cannot seem to get anything right.

All of us who have gone before them have done the same thing. Whether we were carried in our mother's arms or arrived under our own steam, we got into the river of life with Jesus and all his flawed kin. There is not a chance we will be mistaken for one of them. Because we *are* them, thanks be to God, as they are us: Christ's own forever.

# Miracle on the Beach

—

MARK 1:14–20

*As Jesus passed along the Sea of Galilee, he saw Simon and his brother Andrew casting a net into the sea—for they were fishermen. And Jesus said to them, "Follow me and I will make you fish for people." And immediately they left their nets and followed him.*

SOMETIMES I THINK WE MAKE TOO MUCH OF HUMAN volition. The choices we make—about what we will believe and how we will act, about where we will live and whom we will love and what we will do for a living—they are all very important, and we would be crazy to take them lightly, as if they did not really matter. Belonging to God is not a matter of going limp in God's arms, after all. We are called to love, to serve, to heal, to forgive. We are called to imitate Christ, and to make choices that resemble his.

When we agonize too much over them, however, we fall into the ancient trap of works-righteousness—that comfortable old delusion that we can, by our good decisions and good deeds, save ourselves. If we will just work hard enough, we tell ourselves, if we pray enough and help enough and give enough, then God will claim us in the end. Christ will recognize us as his own true disciples because of all the good things we have accomplished. "Well done, thou good and faithful servant."

It is a form of idolatry, and it is peculiarly American, because we *have* so many choices, and because we have had it drilled into our heads that God helps those who help themselves. What we may have lost along the way is a full sense of the power of God— to recruit people who have made terrible choices; to invade the most hapless lives and fill them with light; to sneak up on people who are thinking about lunch, not God, and smack them up side the head with glory.

Take this morning's story, for instance. Most people hear it and right away start worrying about whether they have what it takes to be a disciple. Could you do it? If a clear call were to come to you tomorrow afternoon, could you get up from your chair and walk out the door, without taking your keys or turning off the lights? Could you abandon your grocery cart in front of the frozen food case at the Winn-Dixie and set off for parts unknown without stopping to call home? That is more or less what they did, those first four disciples. Someone they had never seen before in their lives said, "Follow me," and they did, leaving their families, their jobs, their homes behind in order to go with him.

Simon and Andrew had less to lose, apparently. It is a fair guess that they were poor fishermen, since Mark makes no mention of a boat. They cast their nets from the shallows of the sea, and sorted their catch on the beach by themselves. James and John had much more to walk away from: a boat, hired men, their father Zebedee. But rich or poor, both sets of brothers turned away from all the familiars of their lives in order to go after a stranger who called them to follow.

It was not the way such things were done in those days. Rabbis did not seek students; students sought them. Teachers waited for people to come to them and they interviewed them carefully before deciding whether or not to take them on as disciples. Only the most promising students were allowed to stay on, the ones who showed real aptitude for theology. No self-respecting rabbi would ever have gone out to recruit his own followers, and if he had, he would not have picked the first four people he laid eyes on. By doing just that, Jesus set himself apart from the other teachers of his time. He alone walked out among ordinary working people and chose them, without a single question, to be his friends.

But that is not the strangest thing. The strangest thing is that they went along with him. Not one of them or two of them, but all of them. He called and they followed, for which we tend to give them all the credit. What strength, what courage, what faith those four must have had to do what they did, sacrificing everything to go after him! What heroes they were! Well, nonsense. According to Mark, there was nothing hard about it at all. Jesus called and they followed. Period. They did not know him. They were not waiting for him. Chances are they would not have described themselves as religious types, but they took one look at him and that was that. No angst, no torn hearts, no backward glances. They just dropped what was in their hands and went after him, without saying a single word. It was not as if they decided something. It was more like something happened to them, something almost supernaturally beyond their control.

If you ask me, this is not a hero story but a miracle story, as full of God's power as the feeding of the five thousand or the raising of the dead. Listen to the language of miracle stories in Mark: "Be made clean," Jesus said to the leper, and immediately he was made clean (1:41). "Stand up, take your mat and go to your home," he said to the paralyzed man, and the man stood up and immediately took his mat and went home (2:11). "Go, your faith has made you well," he said to the blind man, and immediately

he regained his sight (10:52). "Follow me," Jesus said, and immediately they left their nets and followed him.

Can you hear it? This is no story about the power of human
beings to change their lives, to leave everything behind and follow. This is a story about the power of God—to walk right up to
a quartet of fishermen and work a miracle, creating faith where
there was no faith, creating disciples where there were none just
a moment before.

This is not a story about us. This is a story about God, and
about God's ability not only to call us but also to create us as
people who are able to follow—able to follow because we cannot
take our eyes off the one who calls us, because he interests us
more than anything else in our lives, because he seems to know
what we hunger for and because he seems to be food.

It is a miracle, and to look at it any other way is to deform the
story, twisting it into a tall tale about four courageous fishermen
who sacrificed all to serve their Lord. They did no such thing. If
they did anything under their own power at all, it was simply that
they allowed themselves to fall in love. Jesus showed up, they took
one look at each other, and the rest was history. God acted, and
the disciples let their nets wash out to sea.

And sure, on one level, that moment cost them plenty. They
gave up a lot in that moment, and would lose a lot more before
they were through, but to stress that aspect of the story is to put
the accent on the wrong syllable. Their minds were not on what
they were leaving but on whom they were joining. Their hearts
did not cleave to what was falling from their hands but to what
they were reaching out to find, and in that God-drenched moment of their turning to follow, the miracle occurred: their lives
flowed in the same direction as God's life. Their wills were not
two, three, or four, but one will. Time was fulfilled. The kingdom
came—and comes—every time our own lives are brought into

the same flow, so that we too allow ourselves to fall in love, and follow God, and can do no other.

I am no expert—as Saint Paul says, I have no word from the Lord on this, but if you ask me—then I think sometimes we read this story too narrowly. I am not sure that following Jesus is always a matter of leaving everything behind. That is what it meant for Andrew and Simon and James and John; that is what following meant in their particular lives. But if the story is about being swept into the flow of God's will and giving ourselves over to it, then it seems to me that it will be a different story for every one of us in our own particular lives.

Sometimes following may mean staying at home. It may mean letting the hired servants go and taking care of Zebedee when he gets too old to fish. Sometimes following may mean casting the same old nets in a new way, or for new reasons. It may mean doing something different with the fish you catch, or spending the money they bring at market in a different way. It may mean re-organizing the whole fishing business so that the drifters down at the pier have work to do, and so that everyone who works receives a decent wage. It may mean doing less every day, not more, so that there is time to watch how the light changes on the water, and how the happy fish leap out of it at dusk, happy to have outsmarted you one more time.

The possibilities for following seem endless to me. Sometimes they will be big, no doubt about it, and sometimes they will be too small to mention, but it would be a mistake, I think, to focus too hard on our own parts in the miracle of disciple-ship. The God who called us can be counted on to create us as people who are able to follow. Whenever and however our wills spill into the will of God, time is fulfilled—immediately!—and the kingdom is at hand.

# The Company of Strangers

—

LUKE 4:21–32

*Then Jesus began to say to them, "Today this scripture has
been fulfilled in your hearing." All spoke well of him and were
amazed at the gracious words that came from his mouth. . . .
And he said, "Truly I tell you, no prophet is accepted in the
prophet's hometown."*

SEVERAL YEARS AGO NOW I ATTENDED A WEEKEND
retreat with about seventy other people, where the opening
exercise was to tell a story about someone who had been Christ
for us in our lives. After we had all thought about it a little while,
some people got up to tell their stories to the whole group. There
was one about a friend who stayed put through a long illness
while everyone else deserted, and another one about a neighbor
who took the place of a father who self-destructed. One after the
other, they were stories of comfort, compassion, and rescue. The
conference room turned into a church, where we settled into
the warmth of each other's company. Jesus our friend was there
with us and all was right with the world, until this one woman
stood up and said, "Well, the first thing I thought about when I
tried to think who had been Christ to me was, 'Who in my life has
told me the truth so clearly that I wanted to kill him for it?'"

She burst our bubble, but she was onto something vitally important that most of us would be glad to forget: namely, that the Christ is not only the one who comforts and rescues us. The Christ is also the one who challenges and upsets us, telling us the truth so clearly that we will do appalling things to make him shut up. If you do not believe that, maybe it is because you have not recognized Christ in some of the offensive people God has sent your way. Not all of them, mind you, but some of them—people sent to yank our chains and upset our equilibrium so we do not confuse our own ideas of God with God.

It is easy to do. Some of us built houses in the country because we wanted our chains yanked less often. We left bigger, more complicated places for the simplicity of small town life and we found it here. Others of us grew up here and are not entirely happy with all the changes taking place. Our county is now home to at least four different ethnic groups, not to mention people from all over the United States. More and more trees come down as more and more people move in, and while it is wonderful for the economy, it is scary for the community.

Church is where some of us looked for a smaller group of "like-minded" people. I put that in quotes because we are as different as we can be. One couple who visited here a while back told me they were thinking about joining this church out of sheer curiosity. They said they knew people in this congregation who are on the opposite ends of just about every political issue in the county and they wanted to see for themselves how we kept from killing each other.

One answer, I think, is that we do not ask each other too many questions. For better or worse, we concentrate on what we have in common instead of what separates us. For some people this means keeping secrets about themselves. They learn what they can tell and what they cannot tell. They learn the boundaries of this community, which are wide in some places and narrow in others.

All of us have a secret list of people we would rather not sit next to, here or anywhere else. They may be specific people you can name or they may be certain kinds of people. You know who they are. Some of them are on the list because we are snobs, but others are there because we believe they are sinners. That might not be the word you would use, but it captures the feeling well enough—that there are some people who offend us because we believe they have offended God (who probably would rather not sit next to them either).

It is this whole prickly matter of community that Jesus threatens in his first sermon in Nazareth, and it almost gets him killed. All speak well of him and are amazed at the gracious words that come from his mouth until he begins to attack their sense of community. They want him to do for them what he did in Capernaum. They are his own kin, after all, not a bunch of strangers like the people in Capernaum. He belongs to them. They have a special claim on him which they expect him to honor by doing his best for them.

So far as we know, he did nothing for them but remind them that God's sense of community was bigger than theirs was. He offended them by telling them not one but two stories about how God had passed over them and their kind in order to minister to strangers—first the widow from the wrong side of the tracks in Zarephath and then Naaman the Syrian, who was an officer in the army of Israel's enemies. It was like telling them God had become chaplain to the Ku Klux Klan, or that God had passed over a Sunday school teacher who was sick in order to take care of an ailing Hindu. He was not telling them anything new. He was telling them things that were right there in their own scriptures, only that was not how they used scripture. They used it to close ranks on outsiders, not to open them up, and they snapped shut on Jesus. The minute he denied their special status he went from favorite son to degenerate stranger, who offended them so badly they decided to kill him.

That is how sensitive we are to being told that our enemies are God's friends. That is how mad we get when someone suggests that God loves the people we won't sit next to—the people who disturb and offend us, and who belong to God just as surely as we do. No matter how hard we try, we cannot seem to get God to respect our boundaries. God keeps plowing right through them, inviting us to follow or get out of the way. The problem is not that we are loved any less. The problem is that people we cannot stand are loved just as much as we are, by a God with an upsetting sense of community.

This past week I read a book I cannot stop thinking about, called *The Company of Strangers*. It is by a Quaker theologian named Parker Palmer who is counting on the church to renew public life in this country. For him, the word "public" contains a vision of our interdependence on one another. In public parks, public libraries, and public schools, we come together as strangers who agree to share common resources. We do not have to see eye to eye on everything. We do not even have to like each other. But in order for our public life to work, we do have to respect each other's dignity as human beings, which is what we have in common, and to act with honor among strangers as well as friends. If you and I are walking toward each other on a public sidewalk, our differences do not matter. We make room for each other. We may even nod and say hello. Our community at that point does not depend on our being in agreement with each other about anything except that we will share the sidewalk, where we both belong.

Palmer talks about all the ways public life has broken down in this country, largely because we have begun—for good and bad reasons—to regard strangers as enemies. In a world that grows scarier every day, many of us have retreated to well-defended private lives. We do not go out in public unless we have to. We sort ourselves out into tribes who are suspicious of other tribes and quite often we go to war with one another, either overtly or covertly. The strangers we meet must either be kept out of our lives or made like us, which wreaks havoc with our public life. The endless variety of humankind becomes a threat, not a blessing, and the whole body suffers.

The church is not immune to this sort of thing, but we know better. We *believe* better. We know about Naaman the Syrian and the widow of Zarephath. We know about Jesus himself, who preferred the company of misfits to that of religious people. We believe in a Lord who cares for the stranger and who comes to us as a stranger, reminding us over and over again that while he is with us he does not belong to us. In the church, we are dared to believe that it is God who makes us a community and not we ourselves, and that our differences are God's best tools for opening us up to the truth that is bigger than we are.

The truth is always more than any one of us can grasp all by ourselves. It takes a world full of strangers and friends to tell us the parts we cannot see, and sometimes we want to kill them for it. Jesus' own people tried to kill him, more than once. But he passed through the midst of them and went on his way. How did he do that, when they were all ganged up against him? I do not know, but that is how it still works. If we will not listen, he won't try to change our minds. He will pass right through our midst and go away.

# Show Me a Sign

———

JUDGES 6:11–24A

*Then the LORD turned to Gideon and said, "Go in this might of yours and deliver Israel from the hand of Midian; I hereby commission you."*

THE ONLY THING MOST OF US KNOW ABOUT GIDEON is that some friends of his have put Bibles in hotel and motel rooms all over the world. For some of us there is also a vague memory of him blowing a trumpet, but that is about all, or at least that was about all for me until I came upon this morning's story from the book of Judges.

It is a story from Israel's ancient past—before the temple in Jerusalem, before King David, before Israel had any kings at all. Gideon was one of Israel's judges, like Deborah and Samson— charismatic leaders who, by the spirit of God, defended Israel from her enemies and inspired the people with their heroic deeds.

Gideon was no hero at first, however. Like the other judges, his abilities came from God, not from him. It took the visit of an angel and a sign from the Lord to get him going, and even then the angel had to work pretty hard. That is what I like about Gideon—his undisguised queasiness about answering God's call. He was not brave, he kept coming up with reasons why not, and he would not budge without a display of divine fireworks. That is why I like him. If Gideon could get with God's program, then anyone can.

The story of his call begins in a wine press, where he was hiding out from the Midianites. The press was a big vat carved out of a rock in the ground, big enough for several people to tromp grapes in and big enough in this case to thresh wheat. Gideon was down there because every time the Midianites saw something of value, they galloped in on their camels and took it. They were a nomadic tribe who had plagued Israel for generations, and this particular trouble had been going on for seven years. They let the Israelites do all the work, harvesting the grapes, the wheat, the barley, the olives. Then, when everything was piled neatly in baskets, they swooped in and took it all, killing anyone who got in their way.

The general understanding at the time was that God had sanctioned this violence because of Israel's own idolatry, but seven years turned out to be long enough. God sent a parole officer in the form of an angel to show Gideon a way out, only the initial interview did not go well. "The Lord is with you, you mighty warrior." That is how the angel greeted Gideon, who was in no mood either for flattery or religious talk. "But sir," he replied through gritted teeth, "if the Lord is with us, why then has all this happened to us?"

It was as if the angel had said, "Good morning," and Gideon had said, "What's so good about it?" By his definition, the way you know the Lord is with you is that everything is going well: no starving, no hiding out, no Midianites. Gideon wanted the God he had heard miracle stories about, the God of wonderful deeds who brought Israel up from Egypt, not this God who stood by while people were robbed and killed.

To the angel's credit, he did not tell Gideon that his people had brought the hurt on themselves. The angel just agreed that it was time for it to stop and he commissioned Gideon right on the spot. You do it, he said. "Go in this might of yours and deliver Israel from the hand of Midian." Which was not—*not*—what Gideon had in mind. "But, but, but . . . ," he sputtered. *I'm weak, I'm least, I'm small. There must be a hundred Israelites with better qualifications. I just suggested something ought to be done. I didn't volunteer to do it. Honestly, I am not your man. I am the least impressive guy in my family, which is the weakest link in the tribe of Manasseh.*

"But I will be with you," the Lord said, and that was that. Gideon's own qualifications did not matter. All that mattered was his partnership with God, who does not call anyone to do anything without promising to go too. Still, Gideon wanted to make sure it was really God he was dealing with, so he said, "Show me a sign that it is you."

If he had been a New Testament character, he might have gotten into trouble for that, because in Christian scripture people only ask for signs when they do not have faith. In Hebrew scripture, on the other hand, it is perfectly all right to ask for a sign. It is even considered a good idea—to test the spirits, to make sure that what is calling you does not come from the dark side of the moon or your own imagination. So Gideon did what anyone in his position would have done. He asked for a sign, telling the angel to stay put while he went inside his house to fix a meal.

The next part is so arcane that there is no reason why any of us should understand it, but what Gideon wanted to know was how the angel would consume the meal. If his visitor simply ate the goat, the gravy, and the bread, wiped his lips, and said thank you, then Gideon would know he had a fake on his hands. But if the meal burst into flame and was consumed by fire, then he would know it was God. Don't ask me why it had to happen that way. That was just how God ate dinner in those days.

When Gideon came struggling out of his house with all that food, the angel told him to pour it all on a rock. Then the whole feast went up in smoke, and the angel vanished from Gideon's sight. Now *that* is a sign. And what did Gideon do? The sign he had begged for scared him half to death. "Help me, Lord God!" he cried. "For I have seen the angel of the Lord face to face." But the Lord said to him, "Peace be to you; do not fear, you shall not die." Then Gideon built an altar there to the Lord, and called it The Lord is Peace.

You will have to read the book of Judges to find out the rest of the story. (I'll give you a clue: it was not peaceful for the Midianites.) What I want to hold up this morning is grandfather Gideon's legacy to us all. Not just his sassiness in the presence of the Lord, nor his queasiness when the angel called his bluff. Those are important parts of the story, because they remind us we do not have to stop being human in order to start being God's.

But the real beauty of the story, for me, is that Gideon became the sign he asked for. It was not the burned-up meal on the rock—that sign was for Gideon's benefit alone, so he would know who was calling him. The real sign Gideon wanted was relief for his people—an end to the robbing and killing—something he could celebrate at that altar called The Lord is Peace.

God granted him the sign he longed for, only he was it. Gideon was the sign. By answering God's call, he would become it. He would not just ask for it. He would be it and do it. And that is a powerful legacy for all of us who are tired of hiding from the Midianites, who miss God's wonderful deeds, and who ask God to show off by doing something spectacular. I think we had better be careful what we suggest, because there is every chance in the world God will say, "What a splendid idea! I'm all for it; I hereby commission you."

"But, but, but. . . ." That is what Gideon said. What would you say? Not that it matters, because our qualifications are not important and besides, God has a "but" as well. "But I will be with you," God says, and that turns out to be all we need.

# God's Ferris Wheel

LUKE 6:17–26

*Jesus came down with them and stood on a level place, with a*
*great crowd of his disciples and a great multitude of people. . . .*
*Then he looked up at this disciples and said: "Blessed are you*
*who are poor, for yours is the kingdom of God."*

EIGHT YEARS AGO WHEN I WENT TO ISRAEL FOR THE
first time, one of my great curiosities was how the land itself would match up with the Bible stories I had read about it.
How much of Jerusalem could you really see from the Mount of
Olives? Was the Jordan a river or a stream? My curiosity peaked
the day we piled on the bus to go to Tiberias, where tradition
holds that Jesus gave the Sermon on the Mount (according to
Matthew) or the Sermon on the Plain (according to Luke). You
see the problem.

I have read enough to know that each of the gospel writers
chose his geography for a reason. By putting Jesus on a mountain, Matthew wanted us to think of Moses on Mount Sinai.
As Moses gave the law to Israel from on high, so Jesus gave the
gospel from on high too. By putting Jesus on a plain, Luke wanted
us to see how accessible Jesus was—not above but among the
people to whom he spoke. Both of those made sense to me, but

the problem remained. How was the land itself going to reflect these two accounts?

As soon as the bus pulled into the parking lot, I knew. There was a high hill with a chapel on top—the Chapel of the Beatitudes—that had a long, sloping side that swooped down to the sea. The hollow of that hill made a natural amphitheater—a fine, flat place with hills all around to bounce the sound back: a mount and a plain all rolled into one.

According to Luke, Jesus had just spent all night on the mountain praying. Then he came down and stood on the flat part, surrounded by people from all over the place. Some of them were already sold on Jesus and others were still trying to figure him out, but they all wanted something from him.

There were a lot of sick people in the crowd, Luke says. There were a lot of people with crazy looks in their eyes and others who clearly had not eaten for a while. They had heard about Jesus' power—about how all you had to do was get near him and the demons would fly right out of you. If you had a fever, he could make it go away, and if your leg did not work right he could fix it.

If you could just manage to get his attention, then there was no telling what might happen to you. Some even said he could help you set your business straight. There was a story going around that he had walked up to a local fisherman, Simon Peter by name, who had nothing to show for a whole night's work. When Jesus told him to toss his nets back in the water, he did it, and before he knew it he had more fish than he could fit in his boat. There was apparently nothing Jesus could not do. To make contact with him was the first-century equivalent of winning the lottery, or at least that was the word that was going around.

It was why they were all there trying to touch him, which made it even more remarkable that he remained down there on the plain, where they could all get to him—patting him, pulling him, grabbing him, poking him. Anyone else would have hired some bodyguards, but Jesus did not seem to mind, or if he minded, he did not let that stop him from offering himself to all those people. Some of them were really hurting and some of them were just plain greedy, but he did not discriminate among them. He stood among them instead, preaching a silent sermon to them with his presence before he ever opened his mouth to say a word.

But then he did open his mouth, and what came out were the beatitudes—a series of blessings he pronounced on those who were there. The form of speech he used was a common one. Beatitudes are short, two-part affirmations that sum up common knowledge about the good life. "Blessed are they who have good 401 (k) plans, for their old age shall be comfortable." "Blessed are they who floss, for they shall keep their teeth." That sort of thing.

So the *form* of what Jesus said was familiar to his hearers. He said, "Blessed are . . ." and they all got ready for some nuggets of wisdom. But the *content* of what he said rocked them back on their heels. "Blessed are . . . you who are poor? . . . who are hungry? . . . who weep now? Blessed are you when people hate you, and when they exclude you, revile you, and defame you on account of the Son of Man . . . ?"

Hearing this was like drinking from a glass of what looked like lemonade and finding out that it was bug spray instead. It was a shocking substitution of bad things for good things, in which blessedness was equated with the very things people did their best to avoid—poverty, hunger, grief, hatred. In every case, Jesus made those equations even stronger by tacking a reversal of fortune onto them. "Blessed are you who are poor," he said, "for yours is the kingdom of God. Blessed are you who are hungry now, for you will be filled."

In Matthew's gospel, there are nine of these beatitudes. In Luke's gospel there are only four, plus four "woeitudes" that only

Luke seemed to know about. These were mirror images of the beatitudes, in which woe was equated with things that people did their best to achieve—wealth, food, laughter, esteem. In the same way that Jesus made the bad things sound good, he made the good things sound bad. "Woe to you who are rich, for you have received your consolation. Woe to you who are full now, for you will be hungry."

Since we are so used to hearing them by now, it is hard for us to get a sense of their original shock value. Perhaps if I said, "Blessed are you who suffer from cancer, for you shall be made whole," or "Blessed are you whose prayers are not answered, for you shall see God face to face." Perhaps if I said, "Woe to you who drive new cars, for you shall walk on foot," or "Woe to you with college degrees, for you have received your reward."

As you may be able to tell from your reactions to these statements, the impact of the beatitudes has everything to do with who you are. If you happen to be one of the hungry people, then what Jesus is saying sounds like pretty good news. If you happen to be one of the well-fed people, then it sounds like pretty bad news. The words themselves do not change, mind you. They simply sound different depending on who happens to be hearing them.

I think it is fair to say that most of us hear them from the well-fed end of the spectrum. Not many of us walked here today, and if our stomachs are growling it is not because our cupboards are bare. Most of us are rich, by global standards, and some of us are fabulously so. Many of us have worked hard in hopes that people would speak well of us, and when they do not, we take it as a sign that we still have more work to do.

What this means, I am afraid, is that many of us hear the beatitudes and take the high dive into a deep tank of guilt. Not many of us sell all that we own and give it to the poor, I have noticed, but at least we feel bad about what we have. Or else we learn to ignore this passage by putting it into the same file with all the other good Christian advice that no one we know personally has ever followed.

The catch is, the beatitudes are not advice. There is nothing about them that remotely suggests Jesus was telling anyone what he thought they should do. When Jesus is giving advice, it is hard to miss. "Love your enemies, do good to those who hate you, bless those who curse you, pray for those who abuse you." Now *that* is advice—love, do, bless, pray—one imperative after the other, with no distinction between rich or poor, hungry or well-fed. It is the same list for all of them, whether they happen to be weeping or bent over with laughter.

The beatitudes are not like that. In them Jesus does not tell anyone to do anything. Instead, he describes different kinds of people, hoping that his listeners will recognize themselves as one kind or another, and then he makes the same promise to all of them: that the way things are is not the way they will always be. The Ferris wheel will go around, so that those who are swaying at the top, with the wind in their hair and all the world's lights at their feet, will have their turn at the bottom, while those who are down there right now, where all they can see are candy wrappers in the sawdust, will have their chance to touch the stars. It is not advice at all. It is not even judgment. It is simply the truth about the way things work, pronounced by someone who loves everyone on that wheel.

I think it is the blessing and woe language that trips us up on this passage. Whenever we hear words such as "blessing" and "woe," we think "reward" and "punishment." The blessing things must be what he wants us to do and the woe things must be what he does not want us to do, only where does that leave you, exactly? Finding some reason to sit down and sob in hopes you can move from one list to the other? Doing your best to ruin your own reputation so no one will speak well of you? Blessings and woes cannot be manipulated like that. God cannot be manipulated like that. The beatitudes do not tell us what to do. They tell us who we are, and more importantly, they tell us who Jesus is.

When he first said them out loud, everyone heard them in a different way, depending on who they were. Jesus never said who was who. He let them all sort themselves out, but after they had done that, there was no mistaking what Jesus was good for and what he was not.

Anyone who was there that day to win the lottery could go on home. Even if they managed to nab a little bit of his power, it would not help them get on top and stay on top. Jesus was not any good for that. In fact, people who were attached to that were in for some woes, because the way things are is not the way they will always be, and no one gets to stay at the top of the wheel forever. What goes round, comes round. That is not advice. It is not even judgment. It is God's own truth. It is also pure blessedness for those on the bottom, who never really expected to get off the ground.

Although Luke does not say so, I believe it is also pure blessedness for those on top, because there are some vitally important things about human life on earth that you simply cannot see with your feet so far off the ground. To get a good look at them you have to come down, as Jesus did, from the mountain to the plain. Things may not look as pretty from down there. You may see some things that make you cry, but your grief may teach you more than your good fortune ever did.

Neither the going up nor the coming down is under our control, as far as I can tell, but wherever we happen to be, the promise is the same. Blessed are you who loose your grip on the way things are, for God shall lead you in the way things shall be.

# Thin Places

⟶

LUKE 9:28–36

*Now about eight days after these sayings Jesus took with him
Peter and John and James, and went up on the mountain to
pray. And while he was praying, the appearance of his face was
changed, and his clothes became dazzling white.*

WHO CAN TALK ABOUT THE TRANSFIGURATION?
Jesus certainly did not talk about it, and neither did the
three disciples who were with him. According to Luke, "they
kept silent and in those days told no one any of the things they
had seen." You wonder how Luke ever heard about it himself, or
whether he questioned the wisdom of writing it down.

The moment he did, it became public property. All kinds of
people started pawing through it for significance, explaining why
so-and-so was there, why such-and-such said this or that. I guess
that is all we know how to do with an experience that does not fit
any of our categories. We just keep handling it until we wear it
down to where it feels safe to us. We just keep analyzing it until
we can say something intelligent about it.

The truth is that Luke has presented us with an intensely
private moment between Jesus and God, so private that much
of it happened in a cloud. There were witnesses, it is true, but

in spite of the fantastic goings-on it was all they could do to stay awake, as if the Almighty had sifted sleeping powder over their heads to protect them from things they were not equipped to see. What they did see, they misunderstood. They were terrified by it, which may be why they kept silent, and in those days told no one any of the things they had seen.

So I really cannot talk about it. It would seem disrespectful to talk about it, and yet one thing I can talk about is the human fascination with such events. The Bible is full of them: Moses and the burning bush, Jacob and the ladder full of angels, Job and the voice out of the whirlwind. They are all cracked doors between this world and some other, brighter place where God is no absentee landlord but a very palpable presence.

All in all, things do not seem to work that way anymore. Most bushes do not give off the slightest bit of heat, most ladders do not have anyone's footprints on them but our own, and most whirlwinds, when they speak, do not say anything but "whoosh." You will have to ask someone else where God has gone. I don't know, but I do know plenty of people who are in hot pursuit.

They try all kinds of things in hopes of encountering God. They fast, they pray, they go on pilgrimage, they beat drums. Some of them follow ancient spiritual traditions and others make things up as they go along. Some go to seminary and some go to India, but one way or another what they are all after is an experience of the living God. They have had enough explanations—the careful process of mounting dead butterflies on pins. They want to come face to face with the real thing, and they know better than to pack a net.

A couple of summers ago my husband Ed and I went to Ireland. We both have roots there, and we secretly suspect that we may be descended from Druids. It is that Celtic sense of place that is so appealing—of holy trees, holy wells, holy mountains—

"thin places," as the Irish call them—places where the veil between this world and the next is so sheer that it is easy to step through. If you have been there yourself, then you know about the stone rings and sacred springs. There are so many of them in Ireland that plenty of them are not even marked.

You can be walking down an ordinary country lane and all of a sudden see a footpath leading off to the left. Follow it for a couple hundred feet and you come to a little mossy hole full of crystal clear water. It would be easy to mistake it for an ordinary watering hole if it were not for the tidy bank of stones around it, set there hundreds of years ago by people who recognized a "thin place" right there in the middle of a sheep pasture. If you can stop all the racket in your own mind and body, you can sometimes feel it for yourself— a freshness that drenches you as thoroughly as a shower. How it works is a complete mystery, but there is no denying the effect. Simply to stand near it is to experience living water.

By design, Ed and I were in Ireland on the last Sunday of July, known in that country as "Reek Sunday." It is the day on which the Irish pay their respects to Saint Patrick by climbing the mountain that bears his name—Croagh Patrick, a 2510-foot peak in County Mayo overlooking Clew Bay—where Patrick spent forty days praying for Ireland's deliverance from the worship of pagan gods. With that handled, he charmed all the snakes in the land to leap from the summit to their deaths, and the Emerald Isle has been free of snakes ever since. In gratitude for his ministrations, some thirty thousand people climb Patrick's mountain every year. It is an ancient pilgrimage site—another of those "thin places" where the door is cracked between this world and the next.

The climb to the top begins before dawn. People from all over Ireland arrive in the dark, picking their way through the food stands and souvenir stalls that have been set up for the event. Many of them carry a pilgrim's staff—tall saplings stripped of their bark—which they either brought with them from last year or purchased when they arrived. Quite a few are barefoot, since that is the proper way to climb Croagh Patrick. Those who have done it before know what they are in for. About half way up the Croagh, the mud path ends at an expanse of loose, sharp rocks that are guaranteed to draw blood.

Since the climb is considered good penance, a little pain just makes it better. One by one the pilgrims set off, winding their way up the relatively gentle slope at the bottom of the mountain. In the early morning, before the sun is up, so many of them carry lighted torches that they look like lava in reverse. The golden lights move up the mountain in a steady stream that merges, diverges, and merges again. At a dozen points along the way, they spin off into little orbits as the pilgrims circle stone cairns that serve as stations of the cross.

When they reach the summit, they will stand in the fog before a whitewashed chapel with a Plexiglas porch on the front. Inside the porch, elaborately vested clergy will celebrate the mass all day long. The services will be broadcast over loudspeakers and afterwards pilgrims will file through damp corridors below the chapel to receive the sacrament in their own hands. Then, after a breakfast of cold chocolate bars and hot coffee purchased at the top, they will make their way back down the mountain again. If they are lucky, the whole journey will take a little less than four hours.

Being more of a tourist than a pilgrim, I did not arrive until midday. I had plenty of company, however. Thousands of us filed up the mountain as others came down. There were mothers carrying babies and old men with their trousers rolled up to their knees. There were gangs of teenagers who looked as if they should be robbing cars instead, and matrons in print dresses with flowered scarves tied around their heads. Some people carried icons of Saint Patrick in their arms, while others fingered rosaries. One woman on her way down shouted encouragement to the rest of us. "Don't stop till you've reached the top!" she cried. "You're sinners going up, but you'll be saints going down!"

Since I wore shoes I was moving pretty quickly, but every now and then I would get stuck on a narrow stretch behind someone whose feet were bare. Watching those pale, tender soles picking their way through the muck gave me a lump in the throat. When we arrived at the rocks, it got worse. In the first place, we entered a fog that made it difficult to see more than about ten feet ahead; and in the second place, it was all but impossible to walk upright on the rocks. They shifted underfoot like giant marbles, only sharper. Most people leaned over and became four-legged creatures again, finding their way across the jagged boulders with their fingers and toes.

In the process of looking down more than they looked up, some of them lost their way. Others lost their balance and fell. Even if you could not see them for the fog, you could still hear them. First there was the sound of the stones grinding together, followed by a muffled "whump" and a cry of pain. Every now and then a whistle would blow and a crowd of men in orange slickers would lumber past carrying some poor, wounded pilgrim on a stretcher. Seeing this, the rest of us became more attentive to each other. We reached out to steady each other, and swapped advice on which way to go. Some of us even gave our staffs to people who seemed to need them more.

After a couple hours of this, a bunch of us reached the top and stood there with thousands of other people, all of us with our hair plastered against our heads and our clothes soaked from the heavy fog. We had to hunt around for the chapel, which finally shone out of the fog as a white smudge behind the gray. Standing about fifteen feet below it, we watched the priests in their Plexiglas box, presiding over the mass in their immaculate white robes. The celebrant might as well have been reading the minutes of the previous meeting for all the energy in his voice. Our responses were not much better. Then he snapped the huge white host in half and we filed through the corridors beneath the chapel to receive our individual servings of the body of Christ.

I imagine I was not the only person there who experienced this as something of an anticlimax. Looking at the white pressed circle in my hand and then looking at the bloody feet of the person in front of me, I had no trouble at all deciding which one was the real body of Christ.

The "thin place" had done its work. The door between this world and the next had cracked open for a moment, only the light was not all on the other side. Instead, it lit up this side, where a bunch of wet, tired people whose feet hurt were all walking around with faces bright as candles.

It only took about half as long to go down the mountain as it had taken to climb up. When we got to the rocks, the fog had lifted, so that we could see where we were for the first time that day. The blue, blue water of Clew Bay seemed to reach halfway up into the sky. The river of people flowing down the mountain seemed to be pouring into it. Near the bottom, I asked one ruddy-faced teenager in a black leather jacket why he got up so early on a Sunday morning to climb Croagh Patrick. "It's good for the soul!" he shouted, and ran on ahead of me with his bare feet slapping the mud.

There is no shortage of epiphanies in this world. Those of us who have not yet glimpsed the full brightness of the Lord may still behold his glory, reflected all around us as we stand within the cloud.

*Lent*

# Lenten Discipline

LUKE 4:1–13

*Jesus, full of the Holy Spirit, returned from the Jordan and was led by the Spirit in the wilderness, where for forty days he was tempted by the devil.*

D O NOT BOTHER LOOKING FOR LENT IN YOUR BIBLE dictionary, because there was no such thing back then. There is some evidence that early Christians fasted forty hours between Good Friday and Easter, but the custom of spending forty days in prayer and self-denial did not arise until later, when the initial rush of Christian adrenaline was over and believers had gotten very ho-hum about their faith.

When the world did not end as Jesus himself had said it would, his followers stopped expecting so much from God or from themselves. They hung a wooden cross on the wall and settled back into their more or less comfortable routines, remembering their once passionate devotion to God the way they remembered the other enthusiasms of their youth. Oh, to be young again, and to believe everything is possible.

Little by little, Christians became devoted to their comforts instead: the soft couch, the flannel sheets, the leg of lamb roasted with rosemary. These things made them feel safe and cared for—if

not by God, then by themselves. They decided there was no con-
tradiction between being comfortable and being Christian, and
before long it was very hard to pick them out from the population
at large. They no longer distinguished themselves by their bold
love for one another. They did not get arrested for championing
the poor. They blended in. They avoided extremes. They decided
to be nice instead of holy and God moaned out loud.

Hearing that, someone suggested it was time to call Christians
back to their senses, and the Bible offered some clues about how
to do that. Israel spent forty years in the wilderness learning to
trust the Lord. Elijah spent forty days there before hearing the
still, small voice of God on the same mountain where Moses
spent forty days listening to God give the law. There was also
Luke's story about Jesus' own forty days in the wilderness—a
period of preparation between his baptism and his ministry—
during which he was sorely tested by the devil. It was hard. It
was awful. It was necessary, if only for the story. Those of us
who believe it have proof that it is humanly possible to remain
loyal to God.

So the church announced a season of Lent, from the old
English word *lenten*, meaning "spring"—not only a reference to
the season before Easter, but also an invitation to a springtime
for the soul. Forty days to cleanse the system and open the eyes to
what remains when all comfort is gone. Forty days to remember
what it is like to live by the grace of God alone and not by what
we can supply for ourselves.

I think of it as an Outward Bound for the soul. No one has
to sign up for it, but if you do then you give up the illusion that
you are in control of your life. You place yourself in the hands
of strangers who ask you to do foolhardy things, like walk back-
wards over a precipice with nothing but a rope around your waist
or climb a sheer rock face with your fingers and toes. But none of

these is the real test, because while you are doing them you have plenty of people around and lunch in a cooler.

The real test comes when you go "solo." The strangers put you out all by yourself in the middle of nowhere and wish you luck for the next twenty-four hours. That is when you find out who you are. That is when you find out what you really miss and what you really fear. Some people dream about their favorite food. Some long for a safe room with a door to lock and others just wish they had a pillow, but they all find out what their pacifiers are—the habits, substances, or surroundings they use to comfort them-selves, to block out the pain and fear that are normal parts of being human.

Without those things they are suddenly exposed, like some-one addicted to painkillers whose prescription has just run out. It is hard. It is awful. It is necessary, to encounter the world with-out anesthesia, to find out what life is like with no comfort but God. I am convinced that ninety-nine percent of us are addicted to something, whether it is eating, shopping, blaming, or taking care of other people. The simplest definition of an addiction is anything we use to fill the empty place inside of us that belongs to God alone.

That hollowness we sometimes feel is not a sign of something gone wrong. It is the holy of holies inside of us, the uncluttered throne room of the Lord our God. Nothing on earth can fill it, but that does not stop us from trying. Whenever we start feel-ing too empty inside, we stick our pacifiers into our mouths and suck for all we are worth. They do not nourish us, but at least they plug the hole.

To enter the wilderness is to leave them behind, and nothing is too small to give up. Even a chocolate bar will do. For forty days, simply pay attention to how often your mind travels in that direction. Ask yourself why it happens when it happens. What is going on when you start craving a Mars bar? Are you hungry? Well, what is wrong with being hungry? Are you lonely? What is so bad about being alone? Try sitting with the feeling instead of fixing it and see what you find out.

Chances are you will hear a voice in your head that keeps warning you what will happen if you give up your pacifier. "You'll starve. You'll go nuts. You won't be you anymore." If that does not work, the voice will move to level two: "That's not a pacifier. That's a power tool. Can't you tell the difference?" If you do not fall for that one, there is always level three: "If God really loves you, you can do whatever you want. Why waste your time on this dumb exercise?"

If you do not know whom that voice belongs to, read Luke's story again. Then tell the devil to get lost and decide what you will do for Lent. Better yet, decide whose you will be. Worship the Lord your God and serve no one else. Expect great things, from God and from yourself. Believe that everything is possible. Why should any of us settle for less?

# Life-Giving Fear

LUKE 13:1–9

*At that very time there were some present who told Jesus*
*about the Galileans whose blood Pilate had mingled with their*
*sacrifices. He asked them, "Do you think that because these*
*Galileans suffered in this way they were worse sinners than all*
*other Galileans? No, I tell you; but unless you repent, you will*
*all perish as they did."*

WHEN I WAS A HOSPITAL CHAPLAIN, THE CALLS I
dreaded most did not come from the emergency room,
the psychiatric ward, or even the morgue. They came from the
pediatric floor, where little babies lay in cribs with bandages
covering half their heads and sweet-faced children pushed IV
poles down the hall. One day I received a call to come sit with a
mother while her five-year-old daughter was in surgery. Earlier in
the week, the girl had been playing with a friend when her head
began to hurt. By the time she found her mother, she could no
longer see. At the hospital, a CAT scan confirmed that a large
tumor was pressing on the girl's optic nerve and she was sched-
uled for surgery as soon as possible.

On the day of the operation, I found her mother sitting under
the fluorescent lights in the waiting room beside an ashtray full

of cigarette butts. She smelled as if she had puffed every one of them, although she was not smoking when I got there. She was staring at a patch of carpet in front of her, with her eyebrows raised in that half-hypnotized look that warned me to move slowly. I sat down beside her. She came to, and after some small talk she told me just how awful it was. She even told me why it had happened.

"It's my punishment," she said, "for smoking these damned cigarettes. God couldn't get my attention any other way, so he made my baby sick." Then she started crying so hard that what she said next came out like a siren: "Now I'm supposed to stop, but I can't stop. I'm going to kill my own child!"

This was hard for me to hear. I decided to forgo reflective listening and concentrate on remedial theology instead. "I don't believe in a God like that," I said. "The God I know wouldn't do something like that." The only problem with my response was that it messed with the mother's world view at the very moment she needed it most. However miserable it made her, she preferred a punishing God to an absent or capricious one. I may have been able to reconcile a loving God with her daughter's brain tumor, but at the moment she could not. If there was something wrong with her daughter, then there had to be a reason. She was even willing to be the reason. At least that way she could get a grip on the catastrophe.

Even those of us who claim to know better react the same way. Calamity strikes and we wonder what we did wrong. We scrutinize our behavior, our relationships, our diets, our beliefs. We hunt for some cause to explain the effect, in hopes that we can stop causing it. What this tells us is that we are less interested in truth than consequences. What we crave, above all, is control over the chaos of our lives.

Luke does not divulge the motive of those who told Jesus about the Galileans whose blood Pilate mingled with their sacrifices. The implication is that those who died deserved what they got, or at least that is the question Jesus intuited. "Do you think that because these Galileans suffered in this way they were worse sinners than all other Galileans?"

It is a tempting equation that solves a lot of problems. 1) It answers the riddle of why bad things happen to good people: they don't. Bad things only happen to bad people. 2) It punishes sinners right out in the open as a warning to everyone. 3) It gives us a God who obeys the laws of physics. For every action, there is an opposite and equal reaction. Any questions?

It is a tempting equation, but Jesus won't go there. "No," he tells the crowd, "but unless you repent, you will all perish as they did." In the south, this is what we call giving with one hand and taking away with the other. *No*, Jesus says, *there is no connection between the suffering and the sin*. Whew. *But unless you repent, you are going to lose some blood too*. Oh.

There is no sense spending too much time trying to decipher this piece of the good news. As far as I can tell, it is not meant to aid reason but to disarm it. In an intervention aimed below his listeners' heads, Jesus touches the panic they have inside of them about all the awful things that are happening around them. They are terrified by those things, for good reason. They have searched their hearts for any bait that might bring disaster sniffing their way. They have lain awake at night making lists of their mistakes.

While Jesus does not honor their illusion that they can protect themselves in this way, he does seem to honor the vulnerability that their fright has opened up in them. It is not a bad thing for them to feel the full fragility of their lives. It is not a bad thing for them to count their breaths in the dark, not if it makes them turn toward the light.

It is that turning he wants for them, which is why he tweaks their fear. *Don't worry about Pilate and all the other things that can come crashing down on your heads, he tells them. Terrible things happen, and you are not always to blame. But don't let that stop you from doing what you are doing. That torn place your fear has opened up inside of you is a holy place. Look around while you are there. Pay attention to what you feel. It may hurt you to stay there and it may hurt you to see, but it is not the kind of hurt that leads to death. It is the kind that leads to life.*

Depending on what you want from God, this may not sound like good news to you. I doubt that it would have sounded like good news to the mother in the waiting room. But for those of us who have discovered that we cannot make life safe nor God tame, it is gospel enough. What we can do is turn our faces to the light. That way, whatever befalls us, we will fall the right way.

# A Tale of Two Heretics

—

JOHN 9:1–38

*As Jesus walked along, he saw a man blind from birth. His disciples asked him, "Rabbi, who sinned, this man or his parents, that he was born blind?" Jesus answered, "Neither this man nor his parents sinned; he was born blind so that God's works might be revealed in him."*

THE STORY OF THE MAN BORN BLIND IS A ONE-ACT play in six scenes, with a large cast of characters, as biblical stories go: there are at least twelve disciples, a crowd of nosy neighbors, some Pharisees, two parents, the man himself, and Jesus. These last two get most of the attention, but it is not the kind either of them wants. The story revolves around them because they are the only so-called sinners in it—the man because he was born blind, which in his day was a sure sign of God's judgment—and Jesus because he broke one of the Ten Commandments by healing the man on the sabbath.

These are the two who make everything else happen, but only the man stays put through the whole story. Jesus puts mud on his eyes and then he disappears. "Go, wash in the pool of Siloam," he says, which means that the man never even sees Jesus' face. The healer vanishes before the cure is complete and it is the last anyone sees of him until the end of the story, when he returns to claim his new disciple.

In between times, the man is on his own. Something powerful has happened to him. He does not have a clue how it worked, what he did to get chosen, or who the man who smeared mud on his eyes really was, but all of sudden those are the things everyone around him wants to know. Like a White House aide who has just received a subpoena from the Grand Jury, he is besieged by reporters who assault him with questions from every side.

How were your eyes opened? Where is the man who did it? How could he do that? What did he do to you? How did he open your eyes? What do you say about him, since he has opened your eyes? Not one living soul said, "Alleluia," or "Thank God!" No one asked him what it was like to see for the first time in his life, or whether the light hurt his eyes. Just "How" and "Who" and "Where" and "What."

They all assume he is mixed up in something unsavory. For all he knows, they are right, but the fact is that he can see for the first time in his life, and that miracle has severely compromised his certainty that he knows anything at all about how the world works. He does not know what to believe about what has happened to him. All he knows is that it *has happened*, and while everyone around him wants to know whether it is right or wrong, those are not the categories that concern him at the moment. The categories that concern him are blind and not blind. If his inquisitors are going to insist that blind is right and not blind is wrong, then he will gladly consent to being wrong.

His answers are timid one-liners at first. "I am the man," he says. "I do not know," he says. "He put mud on my eyes. Then I washed, and now I see." But as the questions go on and on until even his own mama and daddy back quietly into the wings, the man grows both in eloquence and courage, finally answering the Pharisees so sharply that they expel him from the congregation.

"Here is an astonishing thing!" he says to them. "You do not know where he comes from, and yet he opened my eyes. We know that God does not listen to sinners, but he does listen to one who worships him and obeys his will. Never since the world began has it been heard that anyone opened the eyes of a person born blind. If this man were not from God, he could do nothing."

When he says that, everyone in the room stops breathing. A nobody from nowhere who was blind until about forty-five minutes ago has just told the board of elders that they could not see God if God bit them on the nose. They do not let the insult go unreturned, either. They rise to their full height in front of him, look down their unbitten noses into his furious new eyes, and say, "You were born entirely in sins, and are you trying to teach us?" And they drive him out—out of their presence and out of the congregation—because he has just proven himself a heretic.

While his parents and neighbors may consider this a terrible disgrace, it has a happy effect. Another heretic hears about it and comes to see the man born blind—a perfect stranger, as far as the man is concerned. The face is new to him, although there is something familiar about the voice. "Do you believe in the Son of Man?" the stranger asks him, which makes the man wince. It sounds like more of what he has just suffered through, only the voice changes the way the words sound. The question does not sound like an accusation this time, but like an offering, from one heretic to another.

"And who is he, sir?" the man asks the stranger. "Tell me, so that I may believe in him."

"You have seen him," the stranger says, "and the one speaking with you is he."

If you read mysteries, then you know what happens next. There you are with just ten pages to go and you do not have a clue—or you have all the clues, but you still do not know what they mean. And then comes that moment of revelation—just the sound of a familiar voice, maybe, asking the one question that makes sense out of all the other questions, and you know—*you know*—who did it.

"Lord, I believe," the man says, and right then and there he worships Jesus.

He has come a long way. At the beginning of the story, he called Jesus a man, then a prophet, then a man come from God. It is almost as if his vision keeps on improving so that he sees more and more clearly who has given him his sight. Finally he gets the name right, as well as the response. "Lord, I believe."

What is hard to remember is that this confession does not take place in a church before an altar. It does not involve anyone in a clerical collar. It is in no way sanctioned by the community of the faithful, who have spit both of these men out. It happens, instead, outside the bounds of religious society, in complete defiance of its rules, as one heretic confesses faith in another.

And yet here we are reading it in church, claiming it as a story about us—which means, I suppose, that we imagine ourselves in the role of the man born blind. The only problem with that reading, as far as I can tell, is that we still have to decide who the Pharisees are. It is too easy to go on tapping the Jews for that role. Plenty of Jews followed Jesus, who was a Jew himself. Peter, the head of the church, was Jewish, and so were all of the apostles. So "Pharisee" means something other than "Jew."

Since we are in John's gospel here, it helps to know that for him the Pharisees operate sort of like a board of examining chaplains. They are the religious authorities who are devoted to ritual purity and the preservation of the law. They are the keepers of the faith, and—by extension—they are the prosecutors of those who do not keep the faith according to their standards. So if you want to know who today's Pharisees are, here are some questions to ask.

Who are the religious people who follow the traditions of the elders, and who—on the basis of that tradition—believe they can tell the true prophets from the false ones? Who are the guardians of the faith, the fully initiated, law-abiding, pledge-paying, creed-saying, theologically correct people who can spot a heretic a mile away?

According to John, these are the people to watch out for, because they think they can see. Furthermore, they think they can see better than other people, and they are not shy about telling you that you are not really seeing what you think you see, or that what you are seeing is wrong. They do not do this to be mean, either. They do this because they love God and maybe even because they love you too. They are doing it to protect you from believing the wrong things.

There are a lot of astounding things that happen in this world that may or may not have anything to do with the power of God. They may have only to do with the power of the human imagination, or the power of suggestion, or—worse yet—with the power of darkness. What if something is not God and I believe that it is?

That is a good pharisaical question, and the answer is: I will get into trouble. My wrong belief will displease God and place my soul at risk. In official terms, I will become a heretic. But according to the story of the man born blind, there is something worse than wrong belief, and that is wrong disbelief. What if something *is* God and I *don't* believe that it is?

That is the question the Pharisees forgot to ask. They were so sure of everything: that God did not work on Sundays, that Moses was God's only spokesman, that anyone born blind had to be a sinner and ditto for anyone who broke the sabbath, that God did not work through sinners, that God did not work *on* sinners, and that furthermore no one could teach them anything.

Meanwhile, the man born blind, who was not sure about anything—he was the one who eventually saw the light. It was the one and only thing he was absolutely sure about: that he could see. If that made Jesus a heretic, then he sincerely hoped he would be allowed to become one too.

*What if it's not God and I believe? What if it is God and I don't?* I do not know which question the blind man asked himself when Jesus was rubbing mud on his eyes, or whether he was too busy being healed to ask any questions at all, but I do know what he had to say afterwards.

"I do not know whether he is a sinner. One thing I do know, that though I was blind, now I see."

# ✢ Good Friday

*Some readers may recognize the sermons that follow as meditations on Jesus' last seven words from the cross. Those same readers will notice that the words are not in their traditional order. In an effort to maintain the integrity of each gospel's witness, the words from each account have been grouped together.*

# The Voice of Love

MARK 15:25–34

*My God, my God, why have you forsaken me?*

W<small>HERE I LIVE, WAY OUT IN THE COUNTRY, THERE</small> are not many stop lights and there are even fewer street lights. People drive fast, and way too many of them never get where they are going. The side of the road is dotted with crosses marking the places where they died: one covered with pink plastic roses for the grandmother who never saw the stop sign; one with a teddy bear for the four-year-old who was not wearing his seat belt when his father tried to pass the truck. Near my house, there is a plain wooden one with one red rose on it for the motorcyclist who was killed by a local woman blinded by the sun.

All of these are bad enough, but what is even worse is to arrive right after the accident has happened. The traffic is backed up for half a mile, the blue lights are flashing. There are so many cars that it is hard to tell what has happened. That is why traffic is backed up—not because the road is blocked but because people want to know what has happened. They ignore the policeman who motions them to move on. They stare at the crushed vehicles, the broken glass. They look around for victims, or survivors.

Some of them pull over either to help or to gawk. I say gawk, but it is only human—to want to know what has happened, to want to know if someone is hurt. For most of us, it is because we sense how easily it could have been us. I too have slammed on brakes when a stop sign appeared out of nowhere. I too have been blinded by the sun. That could be my car. That could be my body. Next week someone I love could be planting a cross on the piece of scorched earth where I died.

Today the wreck is right here, and we have all decided to pull over. For a little while or a long while, each of us has decided to put aside whatever it was we were supposed to be doing in order to see what has happened here. How did things get so turned around? Why did such a promising life come to such a bloody end? Was there anything anyone could have done to prevent it, or was it meant to be? Him instead of us.

It will defy our understanding, in the end. Those who offer us easy explanations are just in a hurry to go home. They do not want to watch the body being tugged from the car. They do not want to sweep up the glass or talk to the survivors. They just want to file their reports and go home, where no one will say, "Yes, but why *him*, why *this*, why *today*?"

The wreckage of the cross is so hard to understand that Holy Scripture gives us four reports on it—not one gospel but four, in which the same story is told from four different perspectives. They all agree on some things: 1) Jesus died on a cross, at a place called Golgotha. 2) Two other people died the same day in the same way. 3) There was a sign above his head that spelled out the charge against him: "King of the Jews." 4) People were so sure he was not coming down that they divided up his clothes on the spot. 5) He was offered some sour wine before he died. 6) He died, before sundown on the day before the sabbath.

Beyond that, each gospel has its own truth to tell, and the differences are striking. Luke reports a conversation between Jesus and the two men dying with him that the other gospel writers do not mention. John does not say anything about Simon of Cyrene carrying Jesus' cross for a little while, nor does John make any mention of anyone mocking him while he died. Matthew's and Mark's accounts are almost identical, except for a few differences in phrasing, but neither of them says a word about Jesus entrusting his mother to one of his disciples, nor his forgiveness of those who hung him on the cross.

This should not surprise anyone who has ever told a story in the presence of someone else who knows it.

"He was really scared," you say.

"No, he wasn't," the other person says. "He was brave."

"I heard him praying under his breath," you say.

"He wasn't praying. He was rehearsing what he was about to say."

"Well, can we agree that there was a big crowd there that day?"

"I never even looked. I couldn't take my eyes off him."

Different people see different things. Different people interpret what they hear differently, and the Bible respects that—respects it so much that it offers us four distinct views of the cross on this day. Matthew and Mark agree on the first of the seven last words. The next three come from Luke's gospel, and the final three from John's gospel. Each of them shows us a different side of Jesus' death. Each of them shows us a different side of ourselves.

The first word is easily the most awful one. "My God, my God, why have you forsaken me?" Here is a man who was born under a star he may or may not have understood. Whatever else it meant, it meant that God's hand was upon him. He had gifts other people did not have, and from the first moment those people noticed him they could not seem to get enough of him. He was food for those who were hungry. He was medicine for those who were sick to death of business as usual, and they followed him around like children.

Twice in his life he heard a voice from heaven telling him who he was—first at his baptism and later on the mountain where he prayed. "This is my Son, my Beloved," the voice said. Not everyone heard it, but he did, and the love in that voice kept him going when other people might have dropped. When he had been up all night, when there was more to do than he could do, when his best friends missed his point and his enemies hounded him like a swarm of black flies, the love in that voice was his own food, his own medicine. "My Son. My Beloved." The sound of it covered him like a cloak. It was his promise, his reassurance that God's hand was upon him.

And then one day it was gone, just like that. It was the worst possible time, too. People were streaming into Jerusalem for Passover. The high priests were nervous. The Romans were nervous. Even his own disciples were nervous. The air had grown green and still, the way it does before a tornado, only no one knew which way it was coming from. Then Judas left the room with a murderous look in his eye and the first drops of stinging rain began to fall.

When the storm finally broke, it broke fast. There was a last, tortured prayer in Gethsemane ("Abba, Father . . . remove this cup from me . . .") but the cup was still there when the prayer was over. The silence was an answer Jesus accepted, so that he was not startled to hear the mob of excited, angry people approaching in the night. They moved toward him with the confidence of people bearing arms, with Judas in the lead. The kiss was a surprise—such a soft indictment—but after that there were no surprises.

By noon the next day he was panting on a cross, receiving the fury of those whose values he had offended. They worked things he had said to them into their insults, so that his own words came back at him like rocks. Even those who were crucified with him got in on the act. A blasphemer was much worse than a robber, after all. So they insulted him too, filling his ears with filth and hate while he strained—*strained*—to hear the voice of love that had sustained him all his life. If there was ever a day he needed to hear it, if there was ever a day he needed to be reminded who he was—but there was no sound from heaven, no sound at all.

It was that silence, I think, that killed him—not the insults, not the nails, not the slow suffocation, but the silence of the Abba who would not say a word.

"My God, my God, why have you forsaken me?" In at least two accounts, those were the last words he said, although there was one more sound after that—a loud cry—remarkably loud for a man whose lungs were so compromised. It was all he had left in him, and when it came out of him he died.

That is as far as we are allowed to go today. To go further might minimize the awful power of this day. Whatever happens next, there is this wreck to be dealt with, this bloody awful mess. Why him, why this, why today? I wish I knew. All I know is that, because of it, none of us ever has to feel what he felt again. Because he was all alone, and we have his company. At our most hurt, our most frightened, our most forsaken by God, we have this companion who has been there and will be there with us. Nothing we think or do in this state can shock him. Nothing we say can make him turn away. If we say, "Where are you, God? I'm all alone here," he said it first. If all we can do is cry out, he cried out first.

It sounds for all the world like the end of faith. Instead, it is the beginning. This Jesus died talking to his Abba, who would not talk back to him. Is there any other definition of faith? In his suffering, he is the comfort of those who have no comfort. In his abandonment, he is the God of those who have no God. Hearing no voice of love, he cried out, making a sound that—for many—became the voice of love.

# In the Name of Law and Order

LUKE 23:26–34A

*Father, forgive them; for they do not know what they are doing.*

L AST SPRING I TALKED WITH SOMEONE WHO GREW up on a farm about what it was like to raise her own food. "The vegetables were fine," she said. "It was the meat that was hard." Once, she said, when it was time to take a certain calf to the slaughterhouse, the baby became so scared that her father asked someone else to drive so he could ride with it in the back of the trailer. By the time they got where they were going he was in tears, she said, because the calf had licked his arm the whole way.

"Father, forgive them, for they do not know what they are doing." Luke's story of Jesus' death is different from Matthew's and Mark's. In this story, Jesus is never forsaken by God. He is forsaken by humanity instead, and not just any old scum. He is forsaken by some of the most highly evolved human beings on the planet—by Romans whose civilization was the most advanced the world has known and by Jews whose intimacy with God was unparalleled. These are the people who sell him out—not all of them, but some of them. These are the people who drive him to the slaughterhouse, and he licks their arms all the way.

Plenty of us think of Jesus as an innocent victim, but I am not so sure about that. The charges against him were blasphemy and treason. Blasphemy was the church's case against him, because he would not deny being the child of God. Treason was the state's case against him, because he allowed his followers to call him their king. Both church and state feared him because he was stirring up the people. They accused him of subverting religion and undermining the nation, and as far as I can tell they were right on both counts. Within thirty years of his death, Jerusalem lay in ruins and Israel was scattered over the face of the earth. Whatever role his death played in that, he saw it all ahead of time and said it would be so. It was one of the things that got him killed.

So the scandal of his death was not that an innocent man died but that he was killed in the name of justice and faith, by people who believed they were doing the right thing.

Whatever else Caiaphas was, he was the protector of the Jewish people, who were under Rome's thumb. He was appointed high priest by Valerius Gratus, the Roman governor before Pontius Pilate, and he knew what that meant. For fifteen years he had worked with the Romans to keep things running as smoothly as possible. First, so that Jews stayed off crosses and out of jail. And second, because there were clear advantages to working with Rome. The roads were better than they had ever been, the police force was excellent, and Roman troops kept Israel safe from other enemies.

The taxes were terrible, it was true, and no one liked living in occupied territory, but the cost of challenging Rome was much higher than the cost of compromising with Rome. So when Caiaphas heard about the Galilean who was stirring up the people, his mind went into overdrive. Passover was coming, when thousands of Jews from all over the world would pour into Jerusalem. It was a dangerous feast anyway, with Israel celebrating her escape from her old oppressors, the Egyptians. Religious fervor would be running high, along with resentment against her new oppressors, the Romans.

If Caiaphas ignored the reports that were coming to him and let the agitator go on agitating, anything could happen. There could be a revolt. A lot of people could die. No matter how he did the arithmetic, it came out the same: better that one person should die than many. Subtract the agitator, and the whole equation calmed down. Caiaphas was stuck between a rock and a hard place. He was just doing his job.

Pilate, meanwhile, had nothing personal against Jesus. Like Caiaphas, he was responsible for people—both Jews and Romans—who expected him to keep the peace. He worked hard to get along with the local authorities. It was easier for all of them that way. But he also wanted the emperor to know he was doing his job down in Palestine—keeping a subject people in subjection, without pushing the point so hard that they pushed back.

When the Sanhedrin sent Jesus to him, Pilate tried to send him back. The last thing he needed was to get involved in a religious dispute. Then someone mentioned that Jesus was a Galilean, and Pilate had a brainstorm. Herod, the governor of Galilee, was in town for Passover. Let *him* deal with Jesus.

But after playing with Jesus for a while the way a cat plays with a mouse, Herod sent him back to Pilate again. Pilate tried three more times to release him, but when it became clear that the people wanted blood, Pilate acquiesced. There was no sense defending one man if it enraged everyone else. He was stuck between a rock and a hard place. He was just doing his job.

"They did away with God in the name of peace and quietness," writes the British author Dorothy Sayers. They did away with him in the name of law and order, in the defense of scripture and creed. Those were the values Jesus challenged, and those were the values by which he was condemned. He was not killed by vice and corruption. He was killed by piety and due process, but not before he pardoned them both.

"Forgive them," he said, not to them but to God. "They do not know what they are doing." Those who were standing around may have thought it funny, to hear a condemned man granting absolution. They may also have wondered whom he meant: the chilly Romans, the hotheaded Jews, the disappeared disciples, the soldiers with his blood drying under their fingernails? Was he addressing Caiaphas, Pilate, Judas, the thieves on either side of him?

He did not have enough breath left in him to say. The important word was "forgive." It meant that the violence stopped with him. It meant that he did not want anyone punished for his death, especially people who had no clue what they were doing. While they pronounced him guilty, he maintained their innocence. He knew who was really on trial, and he wanted the case dropped.

He would not, in other words, participate in the value systems that were killing him. He hung where he did because he was a threat to both church and state. He upset the balance between and within them. He got in the way of people who were just trying to do their jobs, and their solution was to eliminate him.

Throughout his trial, he refused to play their game, leaving open the possibility of their awakening. By the time they had nailed him to a cross, there was precious little he could do to show them another way, but what he could do, he did. He absolved them, passing up the chance to repay blame with more blame. He licked their arms all the way, so that they walked away from his death forgiven, and many of them in tears.

# The Man in the Middle

LUKE 23:35−43

*Today you will be with me in Paradise.*

ALL OVER THE SOUTH, AND ESPECIALLY DURING THE days before Easter, trios of crosses spring up across the countryside. I passed a new set a couple of weeks ago, on a hillside by the highway. The first time I drove by, there were just three upright posts in the ground—the central one about ten feet high and the other two about six feet. The next time I drove by, the crossbeams had been added. A few days later, they were painted white, and a few days after that a purple cloth flapped in the wind on the central cross.

It was a lot of work for someone. While I was watching it go up, I wondered why the person did not stop with one cross, which would have gotten the same basic message across. But in the weeks since then, I have changed my mind. One cross is not the same message as three crosses. One cross makes a crucifix. Three crosses make a church.

All the gospel writers agree that Jesus did not die alone, although Luke is the only one who reports his conversation with the two who died with him. "Conversation" may be too mild a word, under the circumstances.

It all started after they had been hanging there for a while. Jesus was getting most of the attention from the crowd, perhaps because the sign above his head was more spectacular than the others. "This is the King of the Jews," it said, while those on either side were not even interesting enough to record.

According to Matthew and Mark, they were robbers, but Luke does not even say that much. "Criminals," he calls them, so take your pick: thieves, tax evaders, runaway slaves, mutineers. Whatever they did, one of them did not think it was as bad as what Jesus had done, because he joined the crowd in jeering at him. *Aren't you the Messiah?* he sneered. *I thought you were the Messiah. Everyone says you are the Messiah. So why don't you get us out of here?*

It was not something he said under his breath, either, because the other criminal way over on the other side of Jesus heard him and snapped back. "Do you not fear God?" he said, defending the dying man between them. "We are getting what we deserve for our deeds, but this man has done nothing wrong."

Thus, even on the cross, Jesus was surrounded by controversy, being attacked from one side and defended from the other by two men who were as different as they could be. Luke does not name them, but according to the apocryphal gospel of Nicodemus (which never made it into the Bible), their names were Dismas and Gestas—Dismas being the criminal who defended Jesus and Gestas being the one who would have spit on him if he could have gotten himself turned around right.

One thing I have noticed about dying people is that they become more who they are than they have ever been. The approach of death seems to sap the strength they once had for pretending. Their disguises fall away along with their defenses, until all that is left is this condensed version of themselves, in which the core of the human being is laid bare. Some people become meaner than water moccasins, while others become almost luminous, and it is not always easy to tell ahead of time who will turn out to be whom.

Judging from Gestas' behavior on the cross, I would guess that he had been a bitter man most of his life. Maybe he learned early on that there was no sense hoping for much, since everything he loved would be taken away from him sooner or later. Maybe he really was a thief, who dedicated himself to stealing back what had been stolen from him. However it happened, he did not blame himself. That, plus his losses, would have done him in. So he blamed other people instead, for what they had or had not done to make him who he was.

His death sentence was probably no surprise to him. He had been expecting as much for most of his life, but when it finally came he bore no responsibility for it. Whatever he had done to earn it was not, in his mind, his fault. It was the judge's fault, the jury's fault, the arresting officer's fault, God's fault. It was the fault of the man hanging beside him who—if he really were the Messiah—should have been able to get them all out of this mess.

Dismas, on the other hand, seemed to know what he had done to wind up where he was. ("We are getting what we deserve.") He had a sense of justice, even if it had gone thumbs down on him, and he was willing to own up to his part in the verdict. Who knows what allowed him to do that? Maybe he was one of those half-hearted criminals who are half-relieved to be caught, or maybe he was just a gambler with integrity. When he lost, he did not pull out his pistols and shoot everyone else at the table. He simply lost, with as much dignity as he could muster.

Whatever it was, he seemed to know that the one strong move left to him in his life was to accept responsibility for what he had done and to face the consequences. While Gestas lay tied to the railroad tracks cursing everyone he had ever known in his life, Dismas turned around to face the locomotive and even opened his arms to it.

"Jesus, remember me when you come into your kingdom," he said. The man still had hope! Hanging there as bloody, exhausted, and guilty as he was, he recognized someone who was going further than he was, in whose memory, at least, he might survive. That was all he asked—to be remembered—but he was granted a great deal more. "Truly I tell you," the man in the middle said to him, "today you will be with me in Paradise."

They had hours yet to go before that promise came true, long hours in which Luke reports no more talk between the prisoners. And yet wherever the symbol of the three crosses survives, their conversation continues. Gestas and Dismas both have their say, while Jesus bridges the distance between them—the bitter man and the hopeful one, the lost one and the found.

There may only be one cross here today, but God knows we are all hanging on the other two. Whenever we stand near his, we complete the tableau. One cross makes a crucifix. Three crosses make a church.

# The Commendation

LUKE 23:44–46

*Father, into your hands I commend my spirit.*

ACCORDING TO LUKE, JESUS' DYING WAS NOT ONLY painful to him. It was also painful to the whole creation, which twisted and gasped in its own way as he did on the cross. As his light began to go out, darkness came over the whole land. The sun hid its face and for three hours the world lay sleepless through this unnatural night as Jesus' breath grew shallower and shallower. Finally there was the sound of something ripping—a cloth, a shroud, the sky itself?—followed by a loud voice from the cross: "Father, into your hands I commend my spirit." Then he let out his last breath and every creature left alive learned the meaning of silence.

For Luke, Jesus' last words are not a cry of abandonment but a giving of himself back into the hands that made him. At an ordinary funeral, this is called the commendation. The officiant stands near the body and commends the person who has died to God. "Receive him into the arms of thy mercy, into the blessed rest of everlasting peace, and into the glorious company of the saints in light."

There was no one to do that for Jesus, which may have been

why he did it for himself. He was the rabbi at his own funeral, and at least some of those who heard it were scandalized. He had no business commending himself to God. He was a blasphemer, a heretic, who had presumed upon God's name and trespassed on God's sovereignty. That was why he was being put to death, and scripture was very clear about people like him. According to the book of Deuteronomy, "When someone is convicted of a crime punishable by death and is executed, and you hang him on a tree, his corpse must not remain all night upon the tree; you shall bury him that same day, for anyone hung on a tree is under God's curse" (21:22–23).

He was under God's curse, which rendered his last words absurd. It was as if a murderer were commending himself to the family of the person he had murdered, or a traitor were commending himself to the ruler he had betrayed. As far as the authorities were concerned, this was no funeral service, with time out for the dying person's last delusion. It was an execution, for God's sake, at which the prisoner ought to have been gagged.

But the prisoner was not gagged, and by saying what he did, he shifted the entire context of his death. Until he said it, it looked to everyone as if his life was being taken away from him. His perverse religious cult had been stopped. His sinful scheme had failed. He was on the receiving end of the worst punishment the empire knew how to inflict, which should have made him their victim.

But by saying what he did, he took himself out of their hands. By commending himself to the God whose enemy they said he was, he redefined what was happening to him. He gave away what they thought they were taking away from him, and the whole scene lost its balance. One moment there was a tug of war going on between the good guys and the bad guy. The next moment Jesus simply opened his hands and those who thought they had him nailed fell right on top of each other.

Thus Jesus introduced us to the shocking power of sacrifice, which can turn something that looks for all the world like loss into something that feels for all the world like gain. According to Frederick Buechner, "To sacrifice something is to make it holy by giving it away for love." Even if someone is trying to pry it out of your hands. Even if those standing around you laugh and shout that you have no choice, *you have a choice.* You can still decide how you will let go. You can still open your hands at the last moment and give up what others thought they were taking from you. You can even make it holy by doing it for love.

This miracle can happen anywhere, at any time. Holocaust survivor Victor Frankl says he even saw it in the Nazi death camps, where people were made to stand in line for the ovens. Even there, he says, he watched them exercise choice—some of them turned into wild animals in their fear, while others ministered tenderly to those around them.

They had all suffered, and they were about to suffer more, but some of them would not allow the punishment being inflicted on them to become the meaning of their lives. Even there, with so few choices left, they reserved the right to make their own meaning—and the meaning was what they made out of what was happening to them. It was how they stood there. It was whom they loved while they stood there. It was what they said before they died.

# Mother of the New

*Woman, here is your son.*

IN JOHN'S GOSPEL, JESUS IS NOBODY'S VICTIM. HE
needs no help carrying his cross. No one mocks him as he
hangs on the cross. While he is there, he makes provision for his
mother, says he is thirsty not because he is but in order to fulfill
the scripture, and pronounces his job finished without the loud
cry that all the other evangelists agree on.

In John's gospel, he is in charge all the way. We do not have to
worry about him, then, but we do have to worry about those he
leaves behind. What will happen to the world? Will people ever
understand who he was? What will happen to his disciples? Will
they be able to carry on his work, or will they end up as he has?
What will happen to his mother? In those days, a mother's children were her Medicare, her Social Security, and her pension.

This is Mary's second appearance in John's gospel. The first
was three years ago, when she badgered him about the shortage
of wine at a wedding in Cana of Galilee. "Woman," he said way
back then, "what concern is that to you and to me? My hour has
not yet come." Now, presumably, it has. It is the wine of his blood
that is running out this time, right there where she can smell it.

Fortunately, she is not alone. Her sister is there, along with Mary Magdalene and Mary the wife of Clopas. The beloved disciple is also with her—a man who is never named in John's gospel, although he appears at least five times. Jesus' love for him is the only thing about him that matters, apparently. That is his only identity: that Jesus loves him. We do not even know why.

Perhaps it is his loyalty, since he is the only male disciple standing there. The women are not in nearly as much danger as he is. Since a woman's testimony won't hold up in court, they are not likely to be stopped and questioned, but he is, especially if he looks and sounds like a Galilean.

Where are the others? You will have to ask them. Safe, somewhere. Safe and guilty. This may take a load off Jesus' mind, since he does not have to worry about them, but it may also hurt him as much as the nails do, because they would not follow him all the way. We do not know any of this. All we know is that Jesus concerns himself with those who are there—with his mother, whose face is dissolving in front of him, and the beloved disciple, who has appointed himself her bodyguard.

Although they are near enough to hear him, he does not seem to see them at first. There is a lot going on. The soldiers are dividing up his clothes into four piles: robe, prayer shawl, belt, sandals. Passersby are straining to make out the sign over his head, while the chief priests are arguing that Pilate should change what it says.

But finally Jesus does see them, and when he does, he speaks. First he looks at his mother. "Woman," he says—the same thing he called her before, at the wedding—"Woman, here is your son." Then he looks at the disciple standing beside her and says to him, "Here is your mother." Since his hands are not free, he has to do a lot of work with his eyes, indicating which woman and which man. When he is through, the adoption is final. From that hour, John says, the beloved disciple took Jesus' mother into his own home.

It is a gesture of surpassing sweetness, and yet you have to wonder which way it went. Was Jesus looking out for his mother or for his disciple? Who needed whom more?

That Jesus placed his mother in the care of his disciple is our clue that she is a widow. Although Joseph is mentioned twice by name, he never shows up in John's gospel at all. He has presumably died by the time Jesus reaches adulthood, which makes Mary an 'almana, or widow, whose status depends on the surviving members of her husband's household. When Jesus dies, she will belong to no one. She will be responsible to and for herself.

If she were rich and well-placed, this might be good news to her, but she is not. It is far more likely that she will eat other people's leftovers for the rest of her life, with no father, no husband or son to protect her from the cruel things that people say and do. So it is merciful of Jesus to give her a new son. But it is also merciful of him to give that son a new mother, especially this one. Mary cannot be more than fifty years old when her son is crucified. She is no girl, but she is no crone either.

When the beloved disciple takes her home, and when the other disciples come crawling out from under their rocks, they will find themselves in the presence of someone whose contact with the Holy Spirit has been far more intimate than theirs. She has seen things they have only heard about. She has felt things inside her own body they cannot even imagine. Perhaps that is why she stayed put while they fled. Perhaps that is what let her look full into the ruined face that no one but her (and her new son) could bear to see.

While the principalities and powers believe they are tearing his family apart, Jesus is quietly putting it together again: this mother with this son, this past with this future. Although his enemies will succeed in killing him, he will leave no orphans behind. At the foot of the cross, the mother of the old becomes the mother of the new. The beloved disciple becomes the new beloved son.

# Thirsty for Heaven

———

JOHN 19:28

*I am thirsty.*

ACCORDING TO AT LEAST ONE BIBLICAL SCHOLAR, WE really should not call John's story of Jesus' death a "passion narrative," because "passion" implies suffering and in the fourth gospel it is not Jesus who suffers. As he moves with grace and eloquence toward the hour of his death, it is everyone around him who suffers. Judas is exposed as a traitor and Peter as a coward. Annas passes him off to Caiaphas who passes him off to Pilate. Pilate is afraid of him and tries to let him go, but the temple clergy will not hear of it. "We have no king but the emperor," they say when push comes to shove, revealing themselves for the imperial lap-dogs they are.

Meanwhile Jesus does not beg, does not stumble, does not cry out. In John's story, Jesus knows everything before it happens and he remains stalwart to the end—which is why it is so strange to hear him say "I am thirsty" all of a sudden—like any ordinary human being who has been left out in the sun too long.

Anticipating the question, John has answered it ahead of time by putting the explanation in parentheses. Jesus said what he said in order to fulfill the scripture, John tells us. He did not say it because he was really thirsty. He said it so Psalm 69 would come true: "They gave me poison for food, and for my thirst they gave me vinegar to drink" (69:21).

This was important to John because he wrote near the end of the first century, when things had gotten really bad between the Jews who followed Jesus and those who did not. John's congregation did not need to hear about a Messiah who could not carry his own cross or who wondered out loud where God had gone. They needed to hear about a strong Messiah who was above reproach, and that is the Messiah John told them about—not by making anything up, necessarily, but by how he told the story.

In his gospel, nothing is simply what it seems. Water is never just plain water. It is living water, with currents that go back to creation. Bread is never just plain bread. It is manna from heaven, the bread of angels. Wine is never just plain wine. It is the wine of God's presence, especially when there are rivers of it. It is the sign that God's new age has come to pass.

John loves signs. So when Jesus says "I am thirsty," John is quick to let us know that we are not talking about ordinary dryness here. Jesus is busy fulfilling scripture. Jesus is letting John's congregation—and this one, and anyone else who wants to know—that what is happening to him has been in the works for a long time. He is not some second thought God had when Plan A did not work out. He has been around since the beginning. He was there when the spirit first moved over the face of the waters. He was there before Abraham, before Moses, before Gabriel ever went to pay a visit to Mary.

What is happening to him now is the last act in a very long drama. He is finishing it up now, and he is thirsty for more than sour wine. Having accepted capital punishment for the sin of being human, he is now suffering the consequences of that sin. He is cut off from the waters of life. He has given himself away for love, and this is how it looks: he is not only dehydrated but also drained of divinity, like a reservoir whose dam has been destroyed to save the land from drought. He has chosen it willingly, but at what a cost: that he who turned water into wine, who stilled the storm and walked on water should find himself in such a dry place.

Sour wine will not fix it, but sour wine is what he gets, and if it does not make him cry then it must almost make him laugh. He has always had a hard time making himself understood. When he tried to tell Nicodemus about the miracle of new birth, Nicodemus said, "Can one enter a second time into the mother's womb and be born?" When he tried to tell the woman at the well about living water, she said, "Sir, you have no bucket, and the well is deep." People who take him literally almost always miss his point, so of course they give him sour wine to drink.

He drinks it to fulfill the scripture, but it is not what he is thirsty for. He is thirsty for heaven. He is thirsty for reunion with God, and there is only one way he knows how to get there. "Am I not to drink the cup that the Father has given me?"

"I am thirsty" is what he says, but what he means is, "I am ready."

# It Is Finished

JOHN 19:29–30A

*It is finished.*

IT IS FINISHED. HE IS DEAD. YOU MAY TEST IT ANY way you like: hold a feather under his nose, press your finger against the big vein in his neck, stick a spear into his heart. He is dead. The struggle is over, and the last words he said were, "It is finished."

Back when I was a hospital chaplain, my supervisor taught me that the best way to get a patient to talk was simply to sit down someplace where it looked like I might stay for a while, settle back in my seat, and say, "Tell me about it."

"Tell me about what?" I asked him, and he said, "That's the point. You don't know yet, so don't pretend like you do. Just say, 'Tell me about it,' and the other person will let you know what 'it' is."

It is finished, but what is "it," exactly? Well, the dying, for one thing. There was no lethal injection in Jesus' day. There was no attempt to make execution less painful at all, since that would have cut down on its use as a deterrent. The whole point was to make it hurt as much as possible, and everyone agreed that death by crucifixion was the worst. Seneca, a Roman statesman who

witnessed some first-century executions, wrote that he saw cru-
cifixions of many different types. "Some have their victims with
head down to the ground," he said. "Some impale their private
parts; others stretch out their arms on the gibbet."

Jesus probably died right side up, since all four gospel writers
agree that there was a sign above his head. That being the case, he
probably died of suffocation, as his arms gave out and his lungs
collapsed under the weight of his sinking body. Blood loss is another possibility. Heartbreak is a third. Whatever finally killed
him, it came as a friend and not as an enemy. Death is not painful.
It is the dying that hurts.

Another thing that was finished was the project he had begun,
way back when he first saw what kind of explosion it would take
to break through the rock around the human heart. Teaching
would not do it. Neither would prayer nor the laying on of hands.
If he was going to get through, he had to use something stronger
than all of those, and he had to stake his own life on its success.
Otherwise why should anyone believe him?

Self-annihilating love was the dynamite he chose. "No one
has greater love than this," he said on the last night of his life, "to
lay down one's life for one's friends." Having explained it to his
friends, he then left the room to go do it. Less than twenty-four
hours later, it was finished.

Whether or not he intended it, he finished something else
while he was at it. He finished off the religious system that he
opposed: the temple with its careful division between clean and
unclean; the posturing clergy who pretended to know which was
which; the whole idea that a lamb, or a goat, or a calf was an ac-
ceptable substitute for a surrendered human heart.

During the same hour when he died, the parade of Passover
animals into the temple began. For the rest of the afternoon, their
owners slaughtered them while priests caught the blood and

poured it on the altar. Outside in the courtyard, the corpses were skinned and cleaned according to the law of Moses while Levites sang psalms of praises to God.

So there were two bloody places in Jerusalem that day—Golgotha and the temple—both presided over by religious people who believed they were doing God's will. That was one thing the clergy and the politicians agreed on: that by putting Jesus to death, they were doing God's will. When it was all over, some realized for the first time who the scapegoat had been, and the system that put him to death was doomed. Its tactics were exposed. Its motives were revealed: not to defend God but to defend the system. He was the last lamb of God who would die for the people.

So that was finished too. At least one of the reasons Jesus was killed was to prevent a Jewish revolt, but thirty-something years later the revolt happened anyway. The Romans turned on the Jews. Jerusalem was destroyed, and temple Judaism was over forever.

There was one more thing that was finished that day, and that was the separation between Jesus and God. The distance was mostly physical, according to John, and it was only temporary, but when Jesus gave up his spirit his thirst was slaked. He dove back into the stream of living water from which he had sprung and swam all the way home.

Those whom he left behind saw nothing but his corpse. He was not a teacher anymore. He was a teaching—a window into the depths of God that some could see through and some could not. Those who held out hope for a strong God, a fierce God, a God who would brook no injustice—they looked upon a scene where God was not, while those whose feet Jesus had washed, whose faces he had touched, whose open mouths he had fed as if they were little birds—they looked upon a scene in which God had died for love of them.

He had put his own body between them and those who meant to do them harm. He had demolished the rock around their hearts. He had shown them a dangerous new way to live. It was dark by the time they got him down and found a place to lay him. It was the sabbath, his turn to rest. His part was over. His work was done.

# ✢ Easter and the Great Fifty Days

# The Unnatural Truth

EASTER SUNDAY

JOHN 20:1–18

*Early on the first day of the week, while it was still dark, Mary Magdalene came to the tomb and saw that the stone had been removed from the tomb. So she ran and went to Simon Peter and the other disciple, the one whom Jesus loved, and said to them, "They have taken the Lord out of the tomb, and we do not know where they have laid him."*

THE SUNDAY OF THE RESURRECTION IS NOT ONLY the greatest day of the church year; it is also the only one that is set by the moon. Easter always falls on the first Sunday after the first full moon on or after the spring equinox. As complicated as that sounds, it makes ancient sense, since it means Easter coincides with the greening of the earth. Christ is risen and the whole world comes to life. Sap rises in dormant trees, spring peepers start their peeping, and trumpet lilies spill their sweet smell on the air. The connection is a happy one, guaranteed to renew our faith in the creative power of God.

But it is also a misleading one, because spring is entirely natural. Buy a daffodil bulb in the winter and it looks like nothing in your hands—a small onion, maybe, with its thin skin and scraggly roots. If you have had any experience with bulbs, however, that does not worry you. You know all you have to do is wait. Come springtime it will escape the earth and explode with color, a yellow butterfly of a blossom shedding its cocoon. As miraculous as it is, it is completely natural.

Resurrection, on the other hand, is entirely unnatural. When a human being goes into the ground, that is that. You do not wait around for the person to reappear so you can pick up where you left off—not this side of the grave, anyway. You say good-bye. You pay your respects and you go on with your life as best you can, knowing that the only place springtime happens in a cemetery is on the graves, not in them.

That is all Mary was doing that morning—paying her respects, going to his tomb to convince herself it was all true. It was still dark, but even from a distance she knew something was wrong. She could smell damp earth, cold rock from inside. Someone had moved the stone! Afraid he would become a saint, afraid his tomb would become a shrine, someone had taken him away—God knew where—to a steep cliff, to the town dump. His body was all she had left and now it too was gone.

So she ran and brought two of the others back with her, but once they had satisfied themselves that what she said was true, they left her there weeping. If they tried to lead her away, she refused them. She was like an abandoned pup who had lost her master, staying rooted to the last place he had been without the least idea what to do next.

Even angels could not soften her resolve. They were there when she worked up her nerve to look inside the tomb, sitting where he had lain. "Why are you weeping?" they asked her. "They have taken away my Lord," she answered them, "and I do not know where they have laid him."

It never occurred to her they might be the culprits, apparently, but it was not as if she were thinking clearly. She was operating on automatic pilot, so that when she left the tomb she bumped into the gardener without even seeing him. His only value to her was that he might know the answer to her question. "Sir, if you have carried him away, tell me where you have laid him, and I will take him away."

What did she think she would do—have the gardener lay the body over her shoulders, or pick it up all by herself? It was not a reasonable request, but the gardener did not seem to mind. "Mary," he said to her, and she turned to stare at him. "Rabbouni!" she cried out, "my Teacher!"

"Do not hold on to me," he cautioned her, "because I have not yet ascended to the Father."

It was a peculiar thing for him to say since there is no evidence she was holding on to him in any way. Unless it was what she called him—my Teacher—the old name she used to call him. Maybe he could hear it in her voice, how she wanted him back the way he was so they could go back to the way they were, back to the old life where everything was familiar and not frightening like it was now. "Rabbouni!" she called him, but that was his Friday name, and here it was Sunday—an entirely new day in an entirely new life.

He was not on his way back to her and the others. He was on his way to God, and he was taking the whole world with him. This may be why all the other gospel accounts of the resurrection tell us not to be afraid—because new life is frightening. It is unnatural. To expect a sealed tomb and find one filled with angels, to hunt the past and discover the future, to seek a corpse and find the risen Lord—none of this is natural.

Death is natural. Loss is natural. Grief is natural. But those stones have been rolled away this happy morning, to reveal the highly unnatural truth. By the light of this day, God has planted a seed of life in us that cannot be killed, and if we can remember that then there is nothing we cannot do: move mountains, banish fear, love our enemies, change the world.

The only thing we cannot do is hold on to him. He has asked us please not to do that, because he knows that all in all we would rather keep him with us where we are than let him take us where he is going. Better we should let him hold on to *us*, perhaps. Better we should let him take us into the white hot presence of God, who is not behind us but ahead of us, every step of the way.

# Believing in the Word

―

JOHN 20:19–31

*But Thomas said to them, "Unless I see the mark of the nails in his hands, and put my finger in the mark of the nails and my hand in his side, I will not believe."*

I DON'T KNOW ABOUT YOU, BUT IT ALREADY SEEMS TO me as if Easter happened about a month ago. Week before last, some of us were here every evening, singing psalms, washing feet, sitting in front of a black-draped cross with big lumps in our throats. Then on Sunday, hundreds of people passed through this place to get a look at the empty tomb. Approaching it with some of the same awe and fear as those who first discovered it, we did what they taught us to do in the presence of new life: we renewed our baptismal vows, exchanged God's own peace, shared a simple meal of bread and wine.

Then, for most of us, it was back to business as usual: back to the chores, the news, the income tax. If last year's figures are any indication, about a third of last week's worshipers will show up today. I do not say that as a judgment but as a fact of life. It is hard to sustain the enthusiasm of Easter once Easter is over, once the memory gets further and further away.

No one knew this better than John did. Writing near the end

of the first century, he addressed people who had never seen or heard Jesus in the flesh. Most of them had been born after he died, so the stories they heard came second- or third-hand. There were still some eyewitnesses around, but even those trusty souls were getting on in years. A child who was six years old on that first Easter morning would have been close to seventy by the time John wrote his gospel.

John's problem, which is a continuing problem for the church, was how to encourage people in the faith when Jesus was no longer around to be seen or touched. The story of Thomas gave him a way to do that. By detailing that reluctant disciple's doubt, John took the words right out of our mouths and put them in Thomas' instead, so that each of us has the opportunity to think about how we do (or do not) come to believe.

Thomas was not there the first time Jesus appeared to his disciples. He was the only one of the eleven who was not there, which tells you something about his character. Like Peter, he distinguished himself by saying things no one else would say. When Jesus was bent on going to Lazarus' home in Bethany—deep in enemy territory—and everyone else was trying to talk him out of it, Thomas said, "Let us also go, that we may die with him." When Jesus sat down at the last supper table and told his friends not to be afraid, because they knew the way where he was going, it was Thomas who said, "Lord, we do not know where you are going. How can we know the way?"

He was not, in other words, a follower—at least not automatically. He was a brave and literal-minded maverick who could be counted on to do the right thing, but only after he had convinced himself that it *was* the right thing. Maybe you have known someone like that yourself—someone whose refusal to go along with the crowd has more integrity to it than those who go along easily—even when going along is the right thing to do. As it would have been in this case, presumably.

Those who were there that first Easter evening saw the risen Lord. They were so convinced it was him that afterwards they told Thomas he could take their word for it. Jesus was back, still wounded but very much alive. He had forgiven them. He who had every right to hunt them down and punish them for deserting him had not said, "Shame on you," but, "Peace be with you." He had healed them with those words. He had given them back their lives again and made them his partners in the revival of the world. "We have seen the Lord," they told Thomas, in perfect unison, and by all rights his response should have been, "All ten of you saw him at the same time? Well, that's good enough for me. I believe you! What do we do next?"

But that is not, of course, what he said. What he said was, "Unless I see . . . I will not believe," which makes Thomas a stand-in for all of us who want to see something for ourselves before we decide whether or not it is true. I, for instance, have heard some pretty convincing stories about UFO's in my life, but until I see one for myself I will remain a skeptic. I have also heard about stigmata, out-of-body travel, and weeping statues of the Virgin Mary, but so far I have not experienced any of those for myself. Until I do, they remain hearsay for me. I am not saying they are not true. I am saying I do not know them to be true for myself. Unless I see, I will not believe.

It is an understandable attitude. John understood it. Why else would he have told us about Thomas? Even Jesus understood it. In one of his more generous moves, he did not dismiss Thomas from the circle of his friends for failing to trust what the others had told him. On the contrary, Jesus made sure Thomas was included in that circle by coming back and repeating the whole scene a second time for his benefit alone. In the end, no one who was there that night had to take anyone's word for anything. They all saw for themselves, and believed.

That would seem to leave us out—all of us who were not there, who will never lay eyes or hands on the concrete person of Jesus Christ. We are outside the circle of this story by thousands of years and yet Jesus means to include us in it too. Speaking over Thomas' shoulder to the rest of us, he says, "Have you believed because you have seen me? Blessed are those who have not seen and yet have come to believe."

Us, in other words. Those of us who have never seen him in the flesh, who have only the testimony of others to rely on—people who *were* there and who, though they are long dead, still beg us to take their word for what they are sure they saw. They knew they were privileged, that something extraordinary had happened during their lifetimes. They also knew it was up to them to keep it alive somehow, so their children and their children's children could participate in the wonders they themselves had witnessed.

We can thank God they did not do that by reducing Jesus' life to five easy-to-remember slogans and pickling them for all eternity. Instead, they collected all the stories they could remember about him, especially those in which he was most who he was. They wrote them down with all the power still in them, so that when they read them out loud to each other they could feel their hearts beat faster and their palms begin to sweat. They left plenty of the stories intact, even when they found them puzzling or troubling or downright offensive, because they knew those were the ones that stood the best chance of staying alive. People would not be able to leave them alone. They would keep coming back to them over and over again, discovering some fresh new blade of grass each time they did.

If you are a lover of stories, then you know this is true. A good story does not just tell you about something that happened once upon a time. It brings that time back to life so that you can walk around in it and experience it for yourself. You finish an epic like *Gone with the Wind* and you can feel lonely for days, missing Scarlett and Rhett and Melanie. You read James Michener's *Hawaii*—specifically, the chapter about navigating the Strait of Magellan during a storm—and you can get as seasick as any sailor just sitting in your chair. That is the power of the word, and when the word concerns Jesus, that power becomes God's power.

Scripture is the message our ancestors rolled up and put in a bottle for us, because they wanted us to experience the person of Jesus—if not in the flesh, then in the word. Reading what they set down for us all those years ago, we are free to believe it or not. We are free to believe *them* or not, but one thing this morning's story tells us is that seeing is not superior to hearing.

One can trust either sense. One can come to believe either way, but where Jesus is concerned, only a precious few saw him in the flesh, either before or after his resurrection. Millions more have discovered him not in the flesh but in the stories, which have a way of jumping off the page. Rooted in history, they are more than history. Jesus is still alive in them, with power to make us weep, rejoice, hope, act. Maybe that is why we call both him and the stories about him the *living* word of God.

"Put your finger here and see my hands. Reach out your hand and put it in my side." Can we really do that? No. Can the story make us feel as if we can? Yes. If we open ourselves up to it. If we believe, because believing is all the Holy Spirit needs to bring the story to life. Or to put it more precisely, believing is all the Holy Spirit needs to bring us to life, breathing on us the same way Jesus breathed on his disciples.

The story is already alive, with or without us. God wants us to be part of it—to sob on Palm Sunday, to wash each other's feet on Maundy Thursday, to fast on Good Friday, to laugh out loud on Easter Sunday—in these and a thousand other ways, to be part of Jesus Christ's risen life on earth—so that the brave, fragile testimony goes on being heard: "We have seen the Lord!" In the flesh? No. In the story? Possibly. In our life together? Absolutely.

# Hands and Feet

LUKE 24:36B–48

*Jesus said to them, "Why are you frightened, and why do doubts*
*arise in your hearts? Look at my hands and my feet; see that*
*it is I myself. Touch me and see; for a ghost does not have flesh*
*and bones as you see that I have."*

ONE OF THE MOST PECULIAR THINGS ABOUT LUKE'S
resurrection story is the way Jesus identifies himself to his
friends. "Look at my hands and my feet," he says to his frightened,
doubtful disciples. They are shaking in their sandals. They are
wondering if they are having a group hallucination when he offers
them four sure proofs that he is who they think he is: two hands
and two feet, ten fingers and ten toes, which could belong to no
one else but him. It is the wounds he wants them to see, but isn't
it a peculiar way to identify himself? Why not say, "Listen to my
voice" or, "Look at my face?"

Could you identify someone by hands and feet alone? I can see
it now: FBI posters at the post office with hands and feet on them
instead of faces. "Suspect has webbed toes on both feet. Little
toe on left foot appears to have been broken; turns in sharply
at sixty-degree angle. Hands are square, with bitten fingernails.
Small scar on right thumb."

Hands and feet are simply not the first things we notice about one another, and yet they are so telling of who we are. My hands are freckled, like my mother's and my grandmother's. It is the McGahee Irish blood in us. I still have the black spot in my left palm where I accidentally stabbed myself with a sharp pencil in the third grade. There is also a little chunk of my left index finger missing. I was sewing the night Richard Nixon went on national television to talk about Watergate, and when he resigned I was so surprised I cut the end of my finger off. I have a callous on my other hand from all the writing I do and a middle finger that has never been the same since a Tennessee Walking horse pulled it out of joint.

I could tell you the same stories about my feet, only they are more private somehow. Maybe it is because we have acquired the habit of wearing shoes in public, as ladies used to wear gloves. Last week I remarked to someone that most of us have no idea what each other's feet look like, only she begged to differ. Her mother never mastered the knack of photography, she said, and every childhood picture she has of her and her brothers and sisters is from the waist down. When the pictures came back from the drug store, she said, all the kids would huddle around and figure out who was who by the feet. Maybe if we all wore sandals and washed each other's feet as our ancestors did we would know more about what is hidden beneath our shoes. As it is, we know a lot more about each other by our hands.

I could identify some of you by your hands, I think. I have had the privilege of putting brown bread into them over the past two years, and I know some of them by heart. I don't know which ones I like better: the hands with some wear and tear on them, who have some clue what this meal cost, or the little children's hands, who reach out and take it entirely for granted. *This is God's table. I am God's child. Give me my bread.*

What I like about hands is that they do not lie. They can't. We can usually exercise some control over our faces so that they look the way we want them to look, but our hands give us away every time: nervous hands, clenched hands, damp hands, soiled hands. I love those Sherlock Holmes stories where some unsuspecting soul is introduced to Holmes, spends about five minutes in his presence, and leaves the room. Then the great detective turns to Watson and tells him what the visitor does for a living, her family status, income level, and hobbies—all based on having shaken her hand.

Almost twelve years ago now, a dear friend of mine lost his father quite suddenly to a heart attack. By the time he got to the hospital his father had died and that made it even harder to bear. There was no good-bye, no "I love you," no time to get used to the idea of losing him. The first chance my friend had to see his father was at the funeral home, where he walked right up to the casket and took one of his father's quiet hands in his own. They were the same shape and size, those two hands—big, competent paws that could fix anything—strong enough to build a porch swing, soft enough to pat a baby to sleep.

His father had been an auto mechanic who took great pride in distinguishing himself from what he called "shade tree mechanics," those backyard amateurs who covered themselves with grease and left spare parts lying around all over the place. He, on the other hand, was a garage mechanic, who plied his trade as carefully as a surgeon. He kept a clean shop, and before he went home at night he scrubbed his hands with a boar's bristle brush, washing away the grime of the day.

But as careful as he was, his hands stayed stained in places, and it was that my friend was looking for. Turning his father's big hand over in his own, he saw the motor oil in the fingerprints, the calouses dark from years of hauling engines, and he smiled. "It's him," he said. "They tried to clean him up, but look, they couldn't. It's my daddy. It's really him."

"Look at my hands and my feet," Jesus said, and when they did they saw everything he had ever been to them. They saw the hands that had broken bread and blessed broiled fish, holding it out to them over and over again. They saw the hands that had pressed pads of mud against a blind man's eyes and taken a dead girl by the hand so that she rose and walked. They saw the hands that danced through the air when he taught, the same hands that reached out to touch a leper without pausing or holding back.

And his feet—the ones that had carried him hundreds of miles, taking his good news to all who were starving for it—into the homes of criminals and corrupt bureaucrats, whom he treated like long-lost kin; into the graveyard where the Gerasene demoniac lived like a wild dog among the dead, whom he freed from his devils forever.

Looking at those feet, they remembered the vulgar woman who had wet them with her tears and dried them with her hair, and Mary, who had sat there quietly protected by him while her sister Martha railed at her to get up and work.

They were wounded now—all of them—the hands that had joined him to other people and the feet that had joined him to the earth. They had holes in them, sore angry-looking bruises that hurt them to look at, only it was important for the disciples to look, because they had never done it before. Earlier, when they had figured out what was coming to those beloved hands and feet, they had fled, hiding themselves away where they could not see the bleeding nor hear the pounding of the hammers.

*Look*, he said to them afterwards, when the danger was past, *You can look at them now*. He wanted them to know he had gone through the danger and not around it, so he told them to look— not at his face, not into his eyes—but at his hands and feet, which told the truth about what had happened to him, which were the only proof he had that he was who he said he was. Some of us wish he had come back all cleaned up, but he did not. He left us something to recognize him by—his hands and feet, just like ours, or almost like ours. You know what *his* said about him. What do ours say about us? Where have they been, whom have they touched, how have they served, what have they proclaimed?

"You are witnesses of these things," he told them before he left them, entrusting the world to their care. When that world looks around for the risen Christ, when they want to know what that means, it is us they look at. Not our pretty faces and not our sincere eyes but our hands and feet—what we have done with them and where we have gone with them. We are witnesses of these things. We still are: the body of Christ.

# Blood of the Martyrs

~

ACTS 6:1–9; 7:2A, 51–60

*While they were stoning Stephen, he prayed, "Lord Jesus, receive my spirit." Then he knelt down and cried out in a loud voice, "Lord, do not hold this sin against them." When he had said this, he died.*

IN THE SIXTH CHAPTER OF ACTS YOU CAN READ ABOUT the shooting-star ministry of Stephen, first deacon of the church and first martyr, who went down in history for being the first ordinary Christian to follow his shepherd to the slaughter. He was not one of the Twelve. He was not even a candidate to replace Judas when that slot came open. (Matthias got the job.) As far as we can tell, he was not anyone's idea of headline material. He was simply a good, faithful man who could be trusted to distribute food to those who were hungry without putting more on one person's plate than another's.

Sometimes I think that if Stephen had been a better deacon he might not have ended up a martyr too. In those days, deacons were meant to be seen and not heard. They were supposed to wait tables so the disciples could devote themselves to the ministry of the word, but making sack lunches for the widows of Jerusalem turned out to be the least of Stephen's gifts. Once he had hands laid on his head, all the grace and power that poured into him spilled over as signs and wonders. Luke does not give us any details. Maybe Stephen really tried to keep a low profile.

Maybe he was just handing someone her lunch one day when he healed her by mistake. Maybe he only meant to stir the soup, not the spirit, but the spirit lit on him. It lit him up, so that some from the synagogue of the Freedmen could not take their eyes off him. They watched him and they listened to him and based on what they saw and heard, they decided he was no friend of God's, because he showed no respect for what God had taught them through Moses.

So they brought charges against him, standing him up before the council and going down their list: disrespect of holy places, disrespect of holy laws, disrespect of holy customs passed down from generation to generation. When they had finished, Luke tells us, there was a moment of exquisite silence, in which all the council members sat looking at Stephen and saw that his face was like the face of an angel.

That part is not in the reading we heard today, nor is the sermon that got Stephen killed. All we heard was his furious conclusion: "You stiff-necked people, uncircumcised in heart and ears, you are forever opposing the Holy Spirit, just as your ancestors used to do." He called them the enemies of God, and it did not take them long to figure out how to absolve themselves of that guilt. They dragged Stephen out of the city and threw rocks at him until he died.

When you put him and Jesus together, it is pretty hard to deny that this is what Christian success looks like: not converting other people to our way of thinking; not having the oldest, prettiest church in town; not even going out of our ways to be kind and generous, but telling the truth so clearly that some people want to kill us for it.

There are problems with that, of course. In the first place, there is Pilate's question: "What is truth?" And in the second place, most of us have known people who believe they are being martyrs when all they are really being is obnoxious. They are the ones who harass you about your faith until you finally tell them please to get lost and then they start moaning about how hard it is to serve the Lord.

Only I do not think real martyrdom works that way. I do not think you can seek it anymore than you can avoid it. I think it just happens sometimes, when people get so wrapped up in living God's life that they forget to protect themselves. They forget to look out for danger, and the next thing they know it is raining rocks.

You know about Stephen, but let me give you some other examples of what I mean, people who have lived and died in our own century for what they believed. Dietrich Bonhoeffer was born in 1906 in Germany, where he grew up to be a pastor in what was called the Confessing Church—one of the few Christian communities that began to make noise when Hitler rose to power in 1933. During his early ministry, Bonhoeffer served churches, wrote books, and organized a new seminary for his denomination. In 1939, he was introduced to a group seeking Hitler's overthrow.

On April 5, 1943, Bonhoeffer was arrested by the Nazis and put in prison in Berlin. When an attempt on Hitler's life failed one year later, documents were discovered that linked Bonhoeffer to the plot. He was taken to Buchenwald concentration camp and then to Schoenberg prison. On Sunday, April 8, 1945, he was concluding a church service when two men came up to him and said, "Prisoner Bonhoeffer, come with us." He was hanged the next day at Flossenburg prison.

Jonathan Myrick Daniels was a twenty-six-year-old seminary

student at the Episcopal Theological Seminary in Cambridge, Massachusetts, when he heard Martin Luther King, Jr., on television one night, asking volunteers to come to Selma, Alabama, to help secure the right of all people to vote. It was March of 1965. Daniels asked his dean for a leave of absence from his studies and went to Hayneville, Alabama, where he landed in jail in August for joining a picket line.

When he and four others were unexpectedly released one hot afternoon, they knew something was wrong. They walked together to a small store near the jail and took refuge inside. Moments later, a sixteen-year-old black girl named Ruby Sales reached the top step into the store when a man with a gun suddenly appeared and started cursing her. Daniels pulled the girl aside and was shot in her stead.

Bonhoeffer and Daniels both have feast days on the Episcopal Church's calendar of saints. Archbishop Oscar Romero does not, although I expect he will soon. Appointed Catholic archbishop in El Salvador in the seventies, he started out an obedient chaplain to the military officers and wealthy landowners who controlled the country. That lasted until the night he looked out his window to see a huge crowd gathering in the streets.

They were poor people, mostly, who had decided to stop dying quietly and start asking loudly for what they and their children needed to live: justice, education, a decent wage. As Archbishop Romero walked among them, government soldiers opened fire and a great many people were killed. Romero was converted that night, and became a powerful advocate for the least among his flock. The officers and landowners called him a traitor, among other things. While he was celebrating a funeral mass for a woman in his congregation, he was shot dead at the altar.

Not everyone is called to be a martyr. Some of us try pretty hard to make sure we are not, but in these Great Fifty Days when we are working on what it means to be Easter people, I think it is important to remember some of those who believed it meant putting something else ahead of their own safety. As best I can tell, none of them had dying as a goal. It was just what happened to them while they were living the fullest lives they knew how and trying to make that same life available to someone besides themselves.

What their murderers found out, over and over again, was that trying to get rid of them by killing them worked about as well as trying to get rid of dandelions by blowing on their puffs. The harder the wind blew, the further the seeds spread.

Some of them blew all the way here, where it is fair to say we are sustained by the blood of the martyrs, as antique as that phrase sounds. Blood has been spilled, for us and for many. We say so every Sunday. We also say that God has turned it into nourishment for us—O mystery of mysteries—so that we, as Easter people, in the communion of Stephen and all the saints, may continue to ponder the miracle of death turning into life.

# Rest for the Land

ROGATION DAY

LEVITICUS 25:1–17

*Six years you shall sow your field, and six years you shall prune your vineyard, and gather in their yield; but in the seventh year there shall be a sabbath of complete rest for the land, a sabbath for the LORD: you shall not sow your field or prune your vineyard. You shall not reap the aftergrowth of your harvest or gather the grapes of your unpruned vine: it shall be a year of complete rest for the land.*

THERE IS NO REASON WHY ANY OF YOU SHOULD know the word "rogation" or why it belongs in church. It is a word left over from the days when farmers were thought to be more essential to life on earth than attorneys, say, or graduate students. It is word left over from those places where children grew up knowing that peanuts grow underground, not on trees, and that eggs start out warm, in nests, before they are ever collected in styrofoam trays and chilled to stop the life in them from growing.

Back when village life was the norm and most parish churches looked out on fields of lush green and high gold, Rogation Days were the three days before Ascension Day when the faithful said special prayers for the fruitfulness of the earth—thanking God for it and begging God for it—because they knew how quickly a sudden storm could ruin a whole field of mown hay, or how thoroughly a cloud of grasshoppers could reduce a crop of new corn to stubble.

These dangers are not as apparent to those of us who live in cities and buy most of our produce in grocery stores. We will no doubt complain about the small, hard peaches this year with no recollection of the late frost that killed most of the peach blossoms in Georgia and South Carolina last March. My husband Ed stayed up three nights in a row stoking fires in the orchard beside our house. On the third night, which was the coldest, I looked out to see him fanning the warm wood smoke into the blooming tree boughs. He had every heat-producing device we owned out there, so that small flames flickered here and there in the dark grass. He had Coleman lanterns under the cherry tree, a kerosene heater under the plum, and under the peach tree, where he was standing, a veritable bonfire of split poplar logs he kept burning all through the night.

So these Rogation Days matter to me, and to my neighbors. I live among farmers, or at least I used to. More and more of them have sold out and become real estate developers instead. They say they can no longer afford the taxes, now that city people like myself have arrived and driven up land prices. Nor can they compete with the huge farming conglomerates that control even local markets. So they either sell out to developers or become developers themselves, as the demand for second homes in our area rises.

Day by day, fields and pastures are paved and subdivided. Banks of rhododendron as tall as trees are bulldozed and acres of old growth forest come down so that cheap houses with vinyl siding can go up. With all the topsoil gone, the red dirt erodes and slides down into our creeks and rivers, where it piles up until the trout cannot live there anymore. I have a creek on my place that is all but choked now. You can stand in the middle of it and shove a pointed stick three feet down through all the loose silt that has collected in it. When I came to this land five years ago, great blue heron fished for trout in that creek. Now both the trout and the herons are gone.

You already know the story, so I won't go through it all again. The bottom line is that the earth is in distress—a lot or a little, depending on your economic and political views. But whether you lean left or right, whether you are an unrepentant industrialist or a militant tree hugger, chances are that you still think of land as a resource—one to be protected or one to be profited from—but either way, as something inert, with no rights or wishes beyond those of its owners.

In popular thought, land is clay in the hands of those who have gained possession of it. The owner says, "Let there be a sub-division," and behold, there is a subdivision. Or the owner says, "No trespassing. Keep out," and lo, there is a private park. It is the will of the owner that determines the use of the land, and it is a rare owner whose thoughts never turn to the dollar value of the land.

That is why the twenty-fifth chapter of Leviticus is so interesting—a little snippet of the law of Moses that overturns all our notions about ownership of land. It is not yours and it never was, God says to the people through Moses. You are all tenant farmers as far as I am concerned, and you have my permission to work the land for six years in a row. Whatever you make of it is yours to keep. You can put up a hundred jars of tomato pickles for your family if you want, or you can sell them at market for a shekel apiece, but on the seventh year, you shall hang it all up.

Park the tractor. Put the tools away. Oil your work boots and put them in the closet, because the seventh year shall be a sabbath of complete rest for the land. There shall be no sowing, no pruning, no gathering into barns. There shall also be no shooing strangers off your property. If some wheat grows up from last year's seed, it is there for anyone who needs it. If some grapes still grow from the unpruned vines, they belong to anyone who is hungry for them—including the wild animals you used to shoot for stealing your fruit.

During the seventh year, they are all welcome to it. *You* are all welcome to it—landowner and servant, plow ox and wild jackal. You are all released from your roles. You are all excused from your work. You are all free to forage together in these wild, overgrown fields and vineyards which—if you will stop and think about it—may remind you of that time before time when you did not live by the sweat of your brow but walked with me in the garden in the cool of the evening.

Like the sabbath itself, this sabbatical year was offered to humankind as a foretaste of heaven. It was meant to be a preview of the world to come, where there would be no more toil, no more striving, no more division between those who had and those who had not. It was a glimpse of the peaceable kingdom, where wild animals grazed side by side with formerly indentured ones who would never feel the sting of a whip again.

It was the vision of an earth in which forests, vineyards, and fields of dirt were as much creatures of God as the human creatures who exercised dominion over them and it was a reminder to those same humans that they were only temporarily in charge—and never for more than six years at a time. On the seventh year, the land itself had a duty to God that they must stand back and allow it to fulfill. The land had a sabbath commandment to follow, with which no human being was supposed to interfere.

We did interfere, of course. Some people grew rich on the black market fruit business during sabbatical years, while others slapped their heads and said they had lost all track of time. Was it really the seventh year again? Already? A little later in Leviticus, Moses warned the people what would happen if they did not allow the land its rest. God would lay waste to it and scatter those who lived upon it, he said. Then, while the people were in exile and the land lay desolate, it would enjoy the sabbath years it had missed (26:34).

It was not a scary enough threat, apparently. While the sabbatical year was briefly observed around the turn of the first millennium, it was largely ignored after that. According to one source I read, it still worries some extreme orthodox groups in Israel, but most of them get around it by arranging a fictitious sale of their land to a friendly Gentile every seven years, farming it as a sub-lessor, and then buying it back again after the sabbatical year is over.

You know why, don't you? Because there is hardly a human being alive who can sit and watch a field, a yard, or even a flower bed "go to waste" for a year. That is what we say about things that have been removed from our control, by the way. We say they are "going to waste," as if their worth depended on our involvement with them. And not only their worth but also our own. In our world, there is not much payoff for sitting back and letting things go. A field full of weeds will not earn anyone's respect. If you want to succeed in this life (whatever your "field" of endeavor), you must spray, you must plow, you must fertilize, you must plant. You must never turn your back. Each year's harvest must be bigger than the last. That is what land and people are for.

According to Moses, God sees things differently. When the fields are lying fallow, when purple morning glories cover last year's cornstalks and the white-tailed deer help themselves to the wild muscadines that have overcome the vineyard—when the people who belong to this land walk through it with straw hats in their hands instead of hoes and discover that the three peaches that survived the frost are sweeter than the thirty they might have saved with their fires—God does not call this "going to waste." God calls this "observing the sabbath," and wonders why human beings are so resistant to it.

What do we think will happen if we rest for a while? Whatever it is, we have been afraid of it for a long time, and what our fear has done is to separate us—from God, from one another, and from this patient, forgiving earth whose sabbaths we have stolen. This land that gives us our food, our water; these trees that clean the air for us to breathe; all these green and growing things that bless our bodies with their beauty—these are not *resources*. They are fellow *creatures*, with their own rights and responsibilities before God. They have their own sacred duties to perform, if only we will let them.

I don't suppose it will ever happen. It never did, except for a couple of hundred years, but it is still the word of the Lord, as much as "Thou shalt not kill" or "Remember the sabbath day, to keep it holy." Sometimes I think God did not say such things with any real expectation that we could or would keep them. I think God said them for the record instead—so we would know who God is and how the world works, whether or not we ever choose to live according to that knowledge.

At the very least, the knowledge we are offered is that the earth does not belong to us. It has its own dignity, its own holiness, its own life in God. When the sabbath comes, it comes for all God's creatures, stopping them right where they are to recognize their kinship under the dominion of one Lord. Each of us was meant to rest in that knowledge on a regular basis, and to let the resting itself prick our dearest beliefs about who we are and what we are supposed to be doing here.

My prayer for each of you during these Rogation Days is that you will run into some tree, some body of water, some rain drop or blade of grass that shouts your name out loud and that you will have the good sense to go over and introduce yourself—in the name of God the Father, God the Son, and God the Holy Spirit.

# He Who Fills All in All

---

ASCENSION DAY

EPHESIANS 1:15–23

*God put this power to work in Christ when he raised him
from the dead and seated him at his right hand in the heavenly
places, far above all rule and authority and power and dominion, and above every name that is named, not only in this age
but also in the age to come.*

ONCE UPON A TIME, IN A LAND FAR AWAY, THERE
was a kingdom called Georgia—not the one I am from, but
one tucked into the Kachkar Mountains east of the Black Sea,
between modern-day Turkey and Russia, where wild geraniums
carpet alpine meadows and the sound of waterfalls is everywhere.
A thousand years ago it was Camelot, rich in everything that
mattered, including the love of God.

Under the patronage of benevolent kings and queens, artists were brought to Georgia from Constantinople to build huge
churches out of local rock. Some of those artists must have come
with the *Hagia Sophia* in mind, because there was nothing modest about their work. Their Byzantine churches were monuments,
full of exquisite arches, frescoes, and stone work, many of which
survive today.

But only as ruins or museums, because the age of Christianity is over in Turkey. The Mongols conquered Georgia in the thirteenth century. Civilization moved west and east. The last baptisms in the Kachkar Mountains took place in the 1800s. Now the area is predominantly Muslim, as is the rest of Turkey. Meanwhile the ancestors of those ancient artists have become farmers, who still pluck old roof tiles and gargoyle parts out of their fields as they plow.

If you go there today, you can find the wrecks of the great churches deep in the countryside, with what is left of their high walls poking up through the canopy of trees like the masts of stranded ships. All the good carvings have been carried away, along with many of the building stones, which local people have quarried for their own houses.

The churches are multipurpose buildings now, serving as soccer fields, sheep pens, garbage dumps. The roofs are gone. So are the doors, the floors, the altars. All that is left are the walls, the graceful arches, and here and there the traces of an old fresco that has somehow survived the years—half a face, with one wide eye looking right at you—one raised arm, the fingers curled in that distinct constellation: it is Christ the Lord, still giving his blessing to a ruined church.

This, for me, is the image hanging over Paul's letter to the Ephesians, that triumphant letter in which he crowns Christ as the ruler of all creation and the church as Christ's body—not two entities but one—God's chosen instrument for the reconciliation of the world. The church shall be a colony of heaven on earth, Paul says, the divine gene pool from which the world shall be recreated in God's image. From the heart of Christ's body shall flow all the transforming love of God—bestowing hope, Paul says, bestowing riches, immeasurable greatness. As God is to Christ, so shall the church be to the world—the means of filling the whole cosmos with the glory of God.

Imagine a four-tiered fountain, if you will, in which God's glory spills over into Christ, and Christ's glory pours into the church, and the church's glory drenches the whole universe. That is what Paul can see, as clear as day—the perfection of creation through the agency of the church. I have been using the future tense out of sheer disbelief, but Paul does not. He uses the past and present tense: "And he has put all things under his feet and has made him the head over all things for the church, which is his body, the fullness of him who fills all in all."

Paul can see it, although as best anyone can tell he wrote this letter from a jail cell, the only light coming from a small square window above his head. His life was coming to a violent end, which he may also have seen, but none of that diminished his sense of God's providence, or of God's confidence in the church. Paul's own experience did not count—at least not the hecklings, the beatings, the arrests. All that counted was the power he felt billowing through his body when he spoke of Christ—the things he said, which surprised even him; the things that happened to those who heard him and believed. In the grip of that power, which turned him into a bolt of God's own lightning, Paul had no doubt about God's ultimate success. God would succeed. God had already succeeded. The world was simply slow to catch on.

*I'll say.* Like most of you, I belong to a church that falls somewhat short of Paul's vision. I do not know why Christians act surprised when we read about our declining numbers in the newspaper. While we argue amongst ourselves about everything from what kind of music we will sing in church to who may marry whom, the next generation walks right past our doors without even looking in. If they are searching at all, they are searching for more than we are offering them—for a place where they may sense the presence of God, among people who show some sign of having been changed by that presence. They are looking for a colony of heaven, and they are not finding it with us.

In a recent interview in *Common Boundary* magazine, novelist Reynolds Price talked about why he, a devoted Christian, does not go to church. Part of it, he says, is disillusionment dating from the civil rights era, when the white southern Christian church, he says, "behaved about as badly as possible." But that is not the only reason.

"The few times I've gone to church in recent years," he says, "I'm immediately asked if I'll coach the Little League team or give a talk on Wednesday night or come to the men's bell-ringing class on Sunday afternoon. Church has become a full-service entertainment facility. It ought to be the place where God lives."

And yet, according to Saint Paul, it still is. The roof may be gone, and there may be sheep grazing in the nave, but Christ is still there—half a face, with one wide eye looking right at us, one hand raised in endless benediction—still giving his blessing to a ruined church. He cannot, or will not, be separated from his body. What God has joined together, let no one put asunder.

Say what you will about the arrogance of supposing that Christ needs the church as much as the church needs Christ. Paul says that we are his consummation, the fullness of him who fills all in all. Without us, his fullness is not full. Without him, we are as good as dead. He may not need us, but he is bound to us in love. We are his elect, Paul says, the executors of God's will for the redemption of the cosmos.

How can we live with this paradox, this painful discontinuity between Paul's vision of our divine nobility and the tawdry truth we know about ourselves? The easiest way, I suppose, would be to decide that Paul was dreaming. It was a glorious dream, but it was still a dream. Or we could decide that he was right—that the church really is Christ's broker on earth—and the sooner we take over the world, the better.

Only I do not think we can afford either of those options, not without betraying our head, who was stuck with the same paradox. He was the ruler of the universe, born in a barn. He was the great high priest, despised by the priesthood of his day. He was the cosmic Christ, hung out on a cross to dry. On what grounds do we, as his body, expect more clarity than was given him?

The difference, of course, is that we have brought most of our problems on ourselves, while he suffered through no fault of his own. What we share with him—that fullness of his in which we take part—is the strenuous mystery of our mixed parentage. We are God's own children, through our blood kinship with Christ. We are also the children of Adam and Eve, with a hereditary craving for forbidden fruit salad. Frisk us and you will find two passports on our persons—one says we are citizens of heaven, the other insists we are taxpayers on earth. It is no excuse for all the trouble we get into, but it does help to explain our spotty record.

What Paul asks us to believe is that our two-ness has already been healed in our oneness in Christ—not that it *will be* healed but that it already *has been* healed—even if we cannot feel it yet, even if there is no startling evidence that it is so. We are still clumping around in a heavy plaster cast, knocking things over and stepping on the cat, but when the cast comes off we shall see for ourselves what has been true all along: that we have been made whole in him, that we are being made whole in him, that we shall be made whole in him who is "above every name that is named, not only in this age but also in the age to come."

Meanwhile, Paul says, he prays that the eyes of our hearts will be opened so that we can see the great power of God at work all around us. Based on my own experience, this is not the kind of stuff that makes headlines, not the way declining membership numbers do. It is just your basic, raising-the-dead kind of stuff that happens in the church all the time.

Like the brain-damaged young man who shows up one Sunday and asks to become a member of the church. As carefully as he tries to hide it, it is clear that he is out of everything—out of food, out of money, out of family to take him in. No one makes a big fuss. Very quietly, someone takes him grocery shopping while someone else finds him a room. Someone else finds out what happened to his disability check while someone else makes an appointment to get his teeth fixed. And do you know what? Years later he is still there, in the front pew on the right, surrounded by his family, the church.

Or like the woman with a recurrent cancer who is told she has six months to live. The church gathers around her and her husband—laying hands on them, bringing them casseroles, cleaning their house. Someone comes up with the idea of giving the woman a foot massage and painting her toenails red, which does more for her spirits than any visit from the pastor. She gives her jewelry away, she lets her driver's license expire, she starts writing poetry again. She prepares to die, but instead, she gets better.

On Christmas Eve she is back in church for the first time in months, with her oxygen tank slung over her shoulder and a clear plastic tube running under her nose. After the first hymn, she makes her way to the lectern to read the lesson from Isaiah. Her tank hisses every five seconds. Every candle in the place glitters in her eyes. "Strengthen the weak hands," she reads, bending her body toward the words, "and make firm the feeble knees. Say to those who are of a fearful heart, 'Be strong, do not fear! Here is your God.'" When she sits down, the congregation knows they have not just *heard* the word of the Lord. They have seen it in action.

I could keep you here all night, but you get the idea. No matter how hard we try in the church, we will always mess some things up. And no matter how badly we mess some things up in the church, other things will keep turning out right, because we are not, thank God, in charge. With the eyes of your heart enlightened, you can usually spot the one who is. Just search for any scrap of the church that is still standing—any place where God is still worshiped, any bunch of faces that are still turned toward the light—and you will see him there bending over them, his hand upraised in endless blessing. It is he who fills all in all, whose fullness has spilled over into us. It is Christ the Lord.

# The Gospel of the Holy Spirit

PENTECOST

ACTS 2:1–11

*When the day of Pentecost had come, they were all together in one place. And suddenly from heaven there came a sound like the rush of a violent wind, and it filled the entire house where they were sitting.*

DID YOU KNOW THE WORD "CONSPIRE" MEANS TO breathe together? Take a breath. Now blow it out again. There! You have just launched a conspiracy. You can hear the word "spirit" in there too—to conspire—to be filled with the same spirit, to be enlivened by the same wind. That is why the word appeals to me, anyhow. What happens between us when we come together to worship God is that the Holy Spirit swoops in and out among us, knitting us together through the songs we sing, the prayers we pray, the breaths we breathe. It can happen with two people and it can happen with two thousand people. It can scare us or comfort us, confuse us or clarify things for us, but as far as I can tell the Holy Spirit never bullies us. We are always free to choose whether or how we will respond.

Now take another breath. If you have studied earth science, then you know that our gorgeous blue-green planet is wrapped in a protective veil we call the atmosphere, which separates the air we breathe from the cold vacuum of outer space. Beneath this veil is all the air that ever was. No cosmic planet-cleaning company comes along every hundred years or so to suck out all the old air and pump in some new. The same ancient air just keeps recirculating, which means that every time any of us breathes we breathe star dust left over from the creation of the earth. We breathe brontosaurus breath and pterodactyl breath. We breathe air that has circulated through the rain forests of Kenya and air that has turned yellow with sulfur over Mexico City. We breathe the same air that Plato breathed, and Mozart and Michelangelo, not to mention Hitler and Lizzie Borden. Every time we breathe, we take in what was once some baby's first breath, or some dying person's last. We take it in, we use it to live, and when we breathe out it carries some of us with it into the next person, or tree, or blue-tailed skink, who uses it to live.

When Jesus let go of his last breath—willingly, we believe, for love of us—that breath hovered in the air in front of him for a moment and then it was set loose on earth. It was such pungent breath—so full of passion, so full of life—that it did not simply dissipate as so many breaths do. It grew, in strength and in volume, until it was a mighty wind, which God sent spinning through an upper room in Jerusalem on the day of Pentecost. God wanted to make sure that Jesus' friends were the inheritors of Jesus' breath, and it worked.

There they were, about a hundred and twenty of them, Luke says, all moping around wondering what they were going to do without Jesus, when they heard a holy hurricane headed their way. Before any of them could defend themselves, that mighty wind had blown through the entire house, striking sparks that burst into flames above their heads, and they were filled up with it—every one of them was filled to the gills with God's own breath. Then something clamped down on them and the air came out of them in languages they did not even know they knew.

Like a room full of bagpipes all going at once, they set up such a racket that they drew a crowd. People from all over the world who were in Jerusalem for the festival of Pentecost came leaning in the windows and pushing through the doors, surprised to hear someone speaking their own language so far from home. Parthians stuck their heads through the door expecting to see other Parthians, and Libyans looked around for other Libyans, but what they saw instead were a bunch of Galileans—rural types from northern Israel dressed in the equivalent of first-century overalls—all of them going on and on about God's mighty acts like a bunch of Ph.D.'s in middle eastern languages.

Before the day was over, the church had grown from one hundred twenty to more than three thousand. Shy people had become bold, scared people had become gutsy, and lost people had found a sure sense of direction. Disciples who had not believed themselves capable of tying their own sandals without Jesus discovered abilities within themselves they never knew they had. When they opened their mouths to speak, they sounded like Jesus. When they laid their hands upon the sick, it was as if Jesus himself had touched them. In short order, they were doing things they had never seen anyone but him do, and there was no explanation for it, except that they had dared to inhale on the day of Pentecost. They had sucked in God's own breath and they had been transformed by it. The Holy Spirit had entered into them the same way it had entered into Mary, the mother of Jesus, and for the same reason. It was time for God to be born again—not in one body this time but in a body of believers who would receive the breath of life from their Lord and pass it on, using their own bodies to distribute the gift.

The book of Acts is the story of their adventures, which is

why I like to think of it as the gospel of the Holy Spirit. In the first four books of the New Testament, we learn the good news of what God did through Jesus Christ. In the book of Acts, we learn the good news of what God did through the Holy Spirit, by performing artificial resuscitation on a room full of well-intentioned bumblers and turning them into a force that changed the history of the world.

The question for me is whether we still believe in a God who acts like that. Do we still believe in a God who blows through closed doors and sets our heads on fire? Do we still believe in a God with power to transform us, both as individuals and as a people, or have we come to an unspoken agreement that our God is pretty old and tired by now, someone to whom we may address our prayer requests but not anyone we really expect to change our lives?

Of all the persons of the Trinity, I suppose the Holy Spirit is the hardest to define. Most of us can at least begin to describe the other two: God the Father, creator of heaven and earth, who makes the sun shine and the rain fall. God the Son, who was human like us: our savior, teacher, helper, and friend. But how would you describe God the Holy Spirit to a five-year-old child? Even Jesus had a hard time with that one. "The Spirit blows where it chooses," he said in John's gospel, "and you hear the sound of it, but you do not know where it comes from or where it goes" (3:8).

There is some very fine teaching available on the Holy Spirit, and I hope none of you is satisfied with it. I hope none of you rests until you have felt the Holy Spirit blow through your own life, rearranging things, opening things up and maybe even setting your own head on fire. There is nothing you can do to make it happen, as far as I know, except to pray "Come, Holy Spirit" every chance you get. If you don't want anything to change in your life, then for heaven's sake don't pray that, but if you are the type of person who likes to stand out on the porch when there is a storm moving through so you can feel the power that is pushing the trees around, then you are probably a good candidate for the Holy Spirit prayer.

Asking for an experience of the Holy Spirit is only half the equation, however. The other half is recognizing it when it comes. On the whole, I find there are a lot of people in the world who say they have never encountered God as Father, Son, or Holy Spirit, but when they start talking about their lives it seems pretty clear to me they have. They just did not know what to call the experience. They did not have a name for it, so they wrote it off to coincidence or ESP or hormones. And maybe that is all it was for them. Each of us has the right to name our own experiences (or not). But just in case you have had some things happen to you that you do not have a name for, I want to suggest some ways I believe the Holy Spirit acts.

One famous way is to give people a sense of new beginning. Say you have been in a bad mood for the last year. It seems as if all you are doing is moving bricks from one pile to another—at work, at home, in your sleep—just moving bricks until you do not care whether it is day or night. Then one of those nights while you are lying awake in your bed, you hear one bird sing outside—just one. Why is that bird singing in the middle of the night? you wonder, and then you realize it is not the middle of the night anymore. It is the edge of morning. The bird chirps again and something inside of you softens. You take a deep breath for the first time in months and your chest opens up. You get a second wind. You can call this anything you want. I call it an act of the Holy Spirit.

Another trademark of the Holy Spirit is to give people a way back into relationship. Maybe this has happened to you. You are estranged from someone you really care about—because of something you said or did or something the other person said or did—it really does not matter which. The point is, you are tired of it, so you start plotting ways to get through. You draft letters, rehearse phone calls, only none of them sounds right. You are still hanging onto your hurt, or your anger, and it keeps leaking through. Then one day for no apparent reason something inside of you says, "Now." You grab the phone, the person says, "Hello?" and the rest is history. Your heart opens and the right words come out. A reunion gets under way. You can call that anything you want. I call it an act of the Holy Spirit.

These intimate encounters are so potent that it is easy to stop with them, but the truth is that the Holy Spirit can work with hundreds of people at the same time. I have seen it happen over and over again in large rooms full of people who have come together to make decisions or seek direction. One by one, they come into the room with their own agendas. Some of them come fearfully, ready to defend themselves. Then someone says a prayer, people begin to talk, and for no apparent reason positions begin to shift. People listen to each other and take each other seriously. They become creative together, coming up with ideas none of them had thought of on their own. It is as if a fresh wind blows through the room and clears everyone's heads. You can call that anything you want. I call it an act of the Holy Spirit.

Once you get the hang of it, the evidence is easier and easier to spot. Whenever two plus two does not equal four but five— whenever you find yourself speaking with eloquence you know you do not have, or offering forgiveness you had not meant to offer—whenever you find yourself taking risks you thought you did not have the courage to take or reaching out to someone you had intended to walk away from—you can be pretty sure that you are learning about the gospel of the Holy Spirit. And more than that, you are taking part in it, breathing in and breathing out, taking God into you and giving God back to the world again, with some of you attached.

Take a breath. Now just keep breathing. This is God's moment-by-moment gift to us. We can call it air or we can call it Holy Spirit. It counts on us to warm it up, to lend it our lives. In return, it promises to fill us with new wind, to set our heads on fire, giving us tongues to speak of things we cannot begin to understand.

Do we still believe in a God who acts like that? More importantly, do we still experience a God who acts like that? I do not know what your answer is, but if you do not have one I hope you will discover one. Join the Gospel of the Holy Spirit Conspiracy and see what happens next.

*⭑* *The Season after Pentecost*

# Three Hands Clapping

—

TRINITY SUNDAY

JOHN 16:5–15

*Nevertheless I tell you the truth: it is to your advantage that
I go away, for if I do not go away, the Advocate will not come
to you; but if I go, I will send him to you.*

STUDENTS OF ZEN BUDDHISM LOVE TO TELL STORIES
about the koans their teachers have given them to aid their
spiritual awakening. These small, impenetrable questions are designed to frustrate the logical mind so that deeper understanding
may take place. "Understanding" may be the wrong word. When
a koan does its work, the result is more an experience than an
understanding. Those on the receiving end say they discover a
level of reality that lies far beyond reason. One famous Zen koan
is "What was the appearance of your face before your parents were
born?" Another is "What is the sound of one hand clapping?"

Students of Christianity have some koans of their own. Many
of Jesus' parables belong in that category, as do sayings such as
"Those who find their life will lose it, and those who lose their
life for my sake will find it" (Matthew 10:39). One of our toughest
koans, however, is not by Jesus but about him. It is the question
of his status in the godhead, and while theologians may look

upon the doctrine of the Trinity as the answer to that question, it remains a logic-buster. Why does one God need three names? How does one God inhabit three forms? How can God be both three and one?

The Bible often compounds the problem by making it sound as if all three operate independently of one another. "Now I am going to him who sent me," Jesus says in the sixteenth chapter of John's gospel. "Nevertheless I tell you the truth: it is to your advantage that I go away, for if I do not go away, the Advocate will not come to you; but if I go, I will send him to you." Finally, he says, "All that the Father has is mine. For this reason I said that he will take what is mine and declare it to you."

*Who are all these people?* How can God the Father be his own son? And if Jesus is God, then whom is he talking to? And where does the Holy Spirit come in? Is that the spirit of God, the spirit of Jesus, or someone else altogether? If they are all one, then why do they come and go at different times, and how can one of them send another of them?

There are orthodox answers to all of these questions, but I have never entirely understood any of them. I accept them as earnest human efforts to describe something that cannot ever be described, which is the nature of God. We would probably be better off if we left that whole subject alone, but if you have ever lain on your back looking up at a summer night's sky full of stars then you know how hard that is to do. You lie there thinking unthinkable things such as what is out there, exactly, where it all stops, and what is beyond that. You lie there wondering who made it and why and where an infinitesimal speck of dust like yourself comes in. After a while you either start making up some answers or else you go inside where it is safe and turn on the television.

In one of his books, Robert Farrar Capon says that when human beings try to describe God we are like a bunch of oysters trying to describe a ballerina. We simply do not have the equipment to understand something so utterly beyond us, but that has never stopped us from trying.

The prophet Isaiah tried: "I saw the Lord sitting on a throne, high and lofty; and the hem of his robe filled the temple. Seraphs were in attendance above him; each had six wings: with two they covered their faces, and with two they covered their feet, and with two they flew" (6:1–2).

John, the writer of Revelation, tried: "At once I was in the spirit, and there in heaven stood a throne, with one seated on the throne! And the one seated there looks like jasper and carnelian, and around the throne is a rainbow that looks like an emerald" (4:2–3).

Believers throughout the centuries have tried to describe God, but very few have been satisfied with their descriptions. Their words turn out to be too frail to do the job. They cannot paint a true portrait of God, because creatures cannot capture their creator any better than a bed of oysters can dance *Swan Lake*. The best any of us has ever been able to do is to describe what the experience of God is like—how it sounds, how it feels, what it reminds us of. Whether the experience originates in the pages of scripture or in the events of our own lives, the best any of us has ever been able to do is simply to confess what it is like when we are in the presence of God.

The problem is that it is rarely the same experience twice in a row. Some days God comes as a judge, walking through our lives wearing white gloves and exposing all the messes we have made. Other days God comes as a shepherd, fending off our enemies and feeding us by hand. Some days God comes as a whirlwind who blows all our certainties away. Other days God comes as a brooding hen who hides us in the shelter of her wings. Some days God comes as a dazzling monarch and other days as a silent servant. If we were to name all the ways God comes to us, the list would go on forever: God the teacher, the challenger, the helper, the stranger; God the lover, the adversary, the yes, the no.

God is many, which is at least one of the mysteries behind the doctrine of the Trinity. That faith statement is our confession that God comes to us in all kinds of ways, as different from one another as they can be. The other mystery is that God is one. There cannot be a fierce God and a loving one, a God of the Old Testament and another of the New. When we experience God in contradictory ways, that is our problem, not God's. We cannot solve it by driving wedges into the divine self. All we can do is decide whether or not to open ourselves up to a God whose freedom and imagination boggle our minds.

Preachers tie themselves into knots trying to explain what all this means. Some explain that the Trinity is like a three leaf clover. Others point to $H_2O$ in its three incarnations as water, ice, and steam. One Trinity Sunday I found a lumpy envelope on the hood of my car. Inside was a Three Musketeers candy bar with a note that read, "All for one and one for three! Happy Trinity!" All I know for sure is that if human beings were created in the image of God, then a) God is wonderfully diverse and b) we are more alike than we think.

Meanwhile, I do not know why we hold ourselves responsible for explaining things that cannot be explained. Perhaps the most faithful sermon on the Trinity is one that sniffs around the edges of the mystery, hunting for something closer to an experience than an understanding. What, for instance, is the sound of three hands clapping?

# The Cheap Cure

INDEPENDENCE DAY

2 KINGS 5:1–15A

*So Naaman went down and immersed himself seven times in the Jordan, according to the man of God; his flesh was restored like the flesh of a young boy, and he was clean.*

I HAVE NEVER SPENT THE FOURTH OF JULY IN NEW York City before, but after the fireworks over the East River last night I believe there is no better place to be. While I watched them, I thought about the Statue of Liberty out there, and Ellis Island, and the hovering spirits of so many immigrants whose children and grandchildren have turned this little spit of land into a hologram of the world.

"Sweet land of liberty." That is what all the fireworks are about. We call it Independence Day but sometimes I wish we would call it Freedom Day, so we could spend a little more time wondering what that word means. What are we free from? What are we free for? How do I know I am really free? Is my sweet liberty strictly a political thing—my freedom to speak, my freedom to vote—or is it a larger concept, one that includes having enough money to do what I want to do, or being able to choose how I will spend my time?

One of the most peculiar things about America, it seems to me, is that we have so much freedom and are still so unwell. As a nation we are strong, but we are not particularly healthy. Our families, our schools, our cities, and our political systems are all showing signs of disease. Beefed up on steroids of wealth and power, we look pretty good from the outside, but the truth is that inside we are feeling a little shaky.

A few minutes ago we heard the story of Naaman the Syrian, whose main claim to fame is that Jesus mentioned him in a sermon once (Luke 4:27). His story is found in the book of Kings, which is just what it sounds like—a history of the kings of Israel, from David to Zedekiah. Naaman shows up about halfway through, in the ninth century before Christ, when Jehoam was king of Israel. Although Israel and her neighbor Aram (which we know as Syria) were frequently at war, they were momentarily at peace. Aram had the better army, however, and Israel knew it. Israel even knew the name of the commander of the Aramean army, since he had beaten up on them more than once. His name was Naaman, which means "pleasant"—an unlikely name for a warrior, perhaps—but even his enemies admitted that Naaman was a great man, whom God had favored in battle. Think Colin Powell, only with one important difference. Naaman did not photograph well. He had leprosy, which was not as big a problem for a Syrian as it might have been for a Jew, but which ate away at Naaman in more ways than one.

He was a national hero, for goodness' sake. He had an office with a view at the Aramean Pentagon. He hobnobbed with heads of state, but there was always that awkward moment when he met people for the first time. Some handled their surprise well, but others stared at him or looked quickly away. He had learned the hard way about shaking hands. It was better to offer a slight bow, he found, with both hands clasped behind his back. That way he did not have to watch the other person decide whether or not to be brave when he held out his scabby hand. He was so tired of seeing the questions register on their faces. *Good Lord, is that stuff contagious? Poor guy. It must be awful to have to deal with that. Why doesn't he just stay home and spare himself the grief?* But their questions were nothing compared to his own. If God favored him, then why was he sick? And why couldn't anyone in Aram make him well?

Naaman's help came from a source he never expected—a young Jewish girl who had been taken captive during one of his military raids on Israel. She was the least of the least in Aram—a slave, a child, a girl. The book of Kings does not even give her a name, but she was the one who led Naaman to his cure. She did not speak directly to him—he was far too scary for that—but she spoke to his wife, whom she served. "If only my Lord were with the prophet who is in Samaria!" she said to her mistress one day. "He would cure him of his leprosy!"

It was a preposterous suggestion. When the king's own physicians had failed to do Naaman any good, he was supposed to go hunting for a faith healer in Israel on the advice of a pre-adolescent serving girl? It was preposterous, but Naaman jumped right on it. If you have ever been that sick yourself then you understand why. Once you run out of respectable doctors, having done everything they said—once you have taken the pills, applied the poultices, practiced the twenty minutes of positive imaging a day and nothing has changed—well, if someone tells you about a clinic in Mexico where a doctor with a degree in veterinary medicine has discovered a substance that works wonders on humans, there is a good chance you will get in your car and go there. It may sound preposterous, but if you really, really want to get well, then you cannot afford to leave any stone unturned—even if the stone turns out to be a holy man in Israel.

As soon as Naaman's wife told him what the serving girl had said, he went to see the king of Aram, who was happy to oblige his star general. "Go then," the king said to him, "and I will send along a letter to the king of Israel." Naaman took the letter and went home to pack. Since he had no idea what a cure for leprosy cost, he emptied his bank account, loading his chariots with seven hundred fifty pounds of silver and one hundred fifty pounds of gold, plus ten sets of fine clothes. Then he kissed his wife goodbye and set off for Israel, where he presented his letter to the king.

"When this letter reaches you," it said, "know that I have sent to you my servant Naaman, that you may cure him of his leprosy." It was a nice gesture, however misguided. The problem was that Naaman's boss, the king of Aram, did not understand about real power. He thought the king of Israel was the man to see—that if there was a cure available in Israel then the king would surely know about it. Only the king did not know about it, because the only kinds of power he had were political power and military power. He did not know one thing about healing power—the power of God—which was why he got so upset when he read the letter.

The first thing he did, before he told anyone what it said, was to grab his royal robe and tear it right down the middle. Then he howled out loud. "Am I God, to give death or life," he said, "that this man sends word to me to cure a man of his leprosy?" It sounded like a trap to him. The king of Aram had asked him to do something he could not do so that Aram would have an excuse to declare war on Israel. It was all politics to him. Politics was all he knew.

Word of the king's distress got around town pretty quickly. When Elisha—the prophet whom the little Jewish serving girl knew about, even though the king of her country did not—when Elisha heard about it, he sent a message to the king. "Why have you torn your clothes?" he asked. "Let him come to me, that he may learn that there is a prophet in Israel."

That may not have been a strange message at the time, but it sounds pretty strange now. Who would think of going to a prophet for a cure? For a prediction about the future, maybe, or for a hair-raising sermon on the righteousness of God, but for help with a skin disease? What a strange idea.

But as I said before, when you really, really want to get well, you will try anything. So Naaman got directions to Elisha's house and went there. Then he lined up all his horses and chariots in the front yard and waited for the prophet to come out. What was the protocol, exactly? Should he approach Elisha or let Elisha approach him? Was he supposed to kneel or something? He hoped not. Kneeling was really out of the question. He would offer a slight bow, with his hands clasped behind his back. "Good sir," he would say, "I am General Naaman, commander of the army of the king of Aram." That should set the proper tone. Then he could soften up a little. "I have heard so much about you. I come with high hopes, and quite a lot of money besides. I am prepared to pay anything you ask for your services."

While Naaman was still rehearsing his speech, the door to Elisha's house opened and a messenger came out. "Go, wash in the Jordan seven times," the man said to Naaman, "and your flesh shall be restored and you shall be clean." Naaman was so surprised that he hardly heard what the man said. What kind of shabby welcome was this? Where was Elisha, the man of God? At the very least, he owed his visitor a seat in the shade and a cup of cool water. Couldn't he even come out of his house and say hello?

Naaman was furious. He had fully expected Elisha to come out to him—there in the yard—to say some grand words, to make some grand gesture, so that Naaman was cured in a spectacle that no one watching would ever forget. Instead, he was being sent away by a messenger, to go splash in the shallow, muddy Jordan River like a five-year-old boy—he! General Naaman, commander of the army of the king of Aram, with nine hundred pounds of gold and silver in his luggage!

It was too much. It was too, too much. "Are not Abana and Pharpar, the rivers of Damascus, better than all the waters of Israel?" he spat out. "Could I not wash in them, and be clean?" Then he turned and went away in a rage.

His servants must have known him pretty well—well enough to know that he was more hurt than mad—because they tiptoed up to him and convinced him to give it a try. *If he had given you something hard to do, you would have done it*, they reasoned with him. *So he gave you something simple. So?*

It was the beginning of Naaman's cure. He was completely emptied out. His royal connections had gotten him nowhere. His reputation had gotten him nowhere. His bags full of money had gotten him nowhere. Elisha would not even come out of the house to meet him, and now he had been given this supremely stupid thing to do—to strip down in front of all his men and take the world's longest bath in a river that barely came up to his knees.

But because he really, really wanted to get well, he did it. He left his clothes and shoes on the bank. He picked his way through the rocks to the deepest part of the river, where the current bumped against his body like soft pillows. The water was greenish and smelled of fish. There was nothing remotely sacred about it. Naaman found a place to kneel and sank down for the first time. It was cold under the water but not on top of it. He did not dare look at his skin. Seven times he made the passage from cold to hot, from river to sun. Each time he rose he sucked air like a newborn. Then he went down again with his eyes wide open so that the sky wrinkled and turned green as the water. He tried not to think of anything but the numbers. By the seventh time, he was winded. He was also very clean. When he looked down at his skin, he saw the flesh of a five-year-old. It was smooth. It was fresh. He was well.

Later on he tried to pay Elisha, but Elisha would not hear of it. *Your money's no good here,* he told Naaman. *God works for free.* So it was a cheap cure. All Naaman had to do was follow directions. All he had to do was empty himself out, abandoning the pretense that who he was or what he was worth could get him what he needed. All he had to do was strip himself down until his hurt flesh was exposed for everyone to see and go play in the water like a little boy. Then God did for him what military victories and kings and bags of money could never do. God restored his flesh. God created him all over again, and he was made new.

I could explain this story to death, but I don't think I will. You may never hear it again on a Fourth of July weekend, but maybe the next time you are saying your prayers for this great, shaky nation of ours, you will remember that great, leprous man Naaman, whose wealth and power turned out to be useless to him in his search for health, and who was ready to trade it all in when God surprised him with a cheap cure that made him truly free.

# Out of the Whirlwind

JOB 38:1–11, 16–18

*Where were you when I laid the foundation of the earth? Tell me, if you have understanding. . . . On what were its bases sunk, or who laid its cornerstone when the morning stars sang together and all the heavenly beings shouted for joy?*

WE DO NOT HEAR MUCH ABOUT JOB IN CHURCH and yet he remains one of the most compelling figures in the Hebrew Bible. It is that unjustified suffering of his that does it. You can read about Moses splitting the Red Sea or Deborah routing the Canaanites and never once think about your own life, but once Job climbs on his dung heap and starts cursing the day he was born, it is hard not to empathize. Everyone has been there, at one time or another, or at least knows someone who has. A devout woman bears twin boys who are soon diagnosed with cystic fibrosis. Her marriage breaks up under the strain. Then she comes down with multiple sclerosis, just short of her fortieth birthday. A tornado rips through a full church on Palm Sunday morning. The roof collapses, burying bodies under broken pews and shattered stained glass. Among those killed is the pastor's five-year-old daughter.

True stories like these make Job our contemporary in a way

few other biblical characters can be. On our behalf, he shakes his fist at God and says, *Where are you and why are you allowing this to happen? If you want to kill us off, then at least make it quick. There is no reason to break all our bones one by one unless you just like the sound of it.*

Job was the man who did everything right and was repaid with suffering every kind of wrong. He was blameless and upright, the Bible tells us. He feared God and turned away from evil. He was also "the greatest of all the people of the east," with a loving wife, ten children, seven thousand sheep, three thousand camels, five hundred pairs of oxen, five hundred donkeys, and enough servants to look after the whole zoo.

His misfortune came about through no fault of his own. Job was quietly minding his business down on earth one day—praying for each of his children by name and making box lunches for the beggars who showed up at his door—when God and the Satan got into a conversation about him in heaven. This Satan was not the devil, as we usually think of him. The idea of an evil being who operates separately from God did not develop in Judaism until a couple of hundred years after Job was written. In Job's time, the Satan was a perfectly respectable member of God's cabinet, a heavenly being who served as divine prosecutor. His name was *ha-satan*, the Accuser, and his job was to bring people to trial when God said so, but only if God said so. He had no power to do anything except the power God gave him.

I am not even sure he meant to get Job in trouble, but that is what happened. One day God called the heavenly beings together and asked the Satan where he had been lately. "Walking around down on earth," the Satan said, and a smile broke over God's face. "Did you see Job while you were there?" God said. "There is no one like him on earth, a blameless and upright man who fears God and turns away from evil."

"Well, begging your pardon sir, but who wouldn't?" the Satan replied. "Every time he turns around you shower new blessings on him. He's rich, he's healthy, he's happily married, he has ten children. With all due respect, sir, he doesn't worship you for nothing. Take all that away from him and he will curse you to your face."

That was what did it. Either because God was so sure the Satan was wrong or because God was afraid the Satan might be right, God gave him permission to test his premise and Job's trial began. In short order, Job lost everything. His oxen, donkeys, and camels were stolen. His servants were killed defending them. His sheep were struck by lightning. His children all died around the supper table when a big wind out of the desert blew the house down on top of them.

Job's response to all of this set him apart from ordinary human beings. God was right. There was no one like Job on earth. In a formal display of grief, Job tore his robe, shaved his head, and lay face down in the dirt. "The LORD gave, and the LORD has taken away," he mumbled in the dirt. "Blessed be the name of the LORD."

But the Satan was not impressed. "That is because you didn't lay a hand on him," the Accuser said to God. "Hurt him—hurt him physically—and he will curse you to your face." God gave his permission, and the Satan made itching sores erupt all over Job's body, from the soles of his feet to the top of his head. Job's wife told him to curse God and die, but Job would not do it. He just picked up a piece of broken pottery to scratch himself with while he sat speechless on his dung heap. Three of his friends came and sat with him for a full week without saying a word. His suffering was so acute it made them speechless too.

Finally Job erupted. In Stephen Mitchell's stormy translation, Job's grief flies off the page. "God damn the day I was born and the night that forced me from the womb," he said. "Why couldn't

I have died as they pulled me out of the dark? Why were there knees to hold me, breasts to keep me alive? If only I had strangled or drowned on my way to the bitter light."[1]

Job pleads his case on and off for thirty-seven chapters. His friends, who were full of compassion for him when he could not say a word, become defensive when he starts railing at God. They tell him he must have done something to deserve it all, since God does not make mistakes. Instead of defending their friend against God, they defend God against their friend. "God is just," they tell him. "Therefore you must be guilty." Only Job knows he is not guilty, and so does God. What is happening to him defies all human logic, which the three friends cannot stand, so they cope with Job's pain by coming up with pious theories to explain it. The more he suffers, the more platitudes they dish up.

Meanwhile, Job circles in on his closing argument. With nothing left to lose, he sits out on his dung heap covered with boils, yelling at God with both fists in the air. "I have done everything you ever asked me to! Why is this happening to me? Answer me!"

Finally, the Lord does just that, speaking to Job out of the whirlwind. "Who is this whose ignorant words smear my design with darkness? Stand up now like a man; I will question you: please, instruct me. Where were you when I planned the earth? Tell me, if you are so wise. Do you know who took its dimensions, measuring its length with a cord? What were its pillars built on? Who laid down its cornerstone, while the morning stars burst out singing and the angels shouted for joy?"

God's rebuttal goes on for four whole chapters, but never does answer Job's question. Job's question was about justice. God's answer is about omnipotence, and as far as I know that is the only answer human beings have ever gotten about why things happen the way they do. God only knows. And none of us is God.

I am told that Virginia Woolf once wrote to a friend, "I read

the Book of Job last night—I don't think God comes well out of
it." The language of the book is so gorgeous that it is hard for me
to take offense, but some people do. They say that in this speech
God is revealed as an arrogant bully who reaches down a thumb
and squashes Job like a bug, and that a God who shows no more
respect than that for human suffering does not deserve the title.
In which case I guess the Satan is right: no one worships God
for nothing.

I prefer to take my cue from Job, who sounds anything but
crushed when it is all over. "I have spoken of the unspeakable
and tried to grasp the infinite," he says to the Lord at the end. "I
had heard of you with my ears; but now my eyes have seen you.
Therefore I will be quiet, comforted that I am dust." Why quiet,
since he never got an answer, and why comforted that he is dust?
Because Job, of all people, saw God face to face and lived to tell
the tale.

It was as if a flea had insisted that the lion upon which it was
riding stop—*stop right now*—and explain why the ride was so
bumpy and hot. The flea roared and roared as loud as it could,
never expecting to be heard, much less answered, until one day
the lion turned around and roared right back, so that the flea saw
itself reflected in both golden eyes at once. Never mind what the
lion said. The lion turned around. The lion roared back. And that
is enough for anyone to live on the rest of his life.

If there is an answer to the problem of unjustified suffering in
Job, then, it is only this: that for most of us, the worst thing that
can happen is not to suffer without reason but to suffer without
God—without any hope of consolation or rebirth. All other pain
pales next to the pain of divine abandonment (ask Jesus about
that), and what Job wants us to know is that God does not finally
abandon us. When there is nothing left—when all the flocks have
been stolen and all the children have been buried—when there

is nothing left but a potsherd with which to scratch our sores, what is still left is the God of all creation, who laid the foundation of the earth, who has walked in the recesses of the deep, who has made Behemoth and Leviathan and everything that breathes. This is the Lord of all life, who never runs out of life, and whom we may always ask for more.

According to Job, we do not have to be polite about it, either. In the end, God prefers Job's outrage to the piety of Job's friends. When in pain, we are allowed to yell as loudly as we can. "Why is this happening to me? Answer me!" Devout defiance pleases God.[2] It may even bring God out of hiding, with a roar that lays our ears back flat against our heads (and makes the angels shout for joy).

### Notes

1. This and all subsequent quotations of Job come from Stephen Mitchell, *The Book of Job* (San Francisco: North Point Press, 1979).

2. With thanks to William Safire for his book *The First Dissident: The Book of Job in Today's Politics* (New York: Random House, 1992).

# Perfect in Weakness

‒

2 CORINTHIANS 12:2–10

*A thorn was given me in the flesh, a messenger of Satan to torment me, to keep me from being too elated. Three times I appealed to the Lord about this, that it would leave me, but he said to me, "My grace is sufficient for you, for power is made perfect in weakness." So, I will boast all the more gladly of my weaknesses, so that the power of Christ may dwell in me.*

SEVERAL YEARS AGO I HEARD A STORY THAT HAS stayed with me, mostly because I do not understand it. It is a true story, about a woman whose life was coming apart at the seams. When one of her friends told her about a silent retreat at a nearby convent, she decided to give it a try. She had never done anything like that before.

Once she arrived, she received her room assignment and was standing in the dormitory elevator with her suitcase in her hand when a short, plump nun stepped inside with her. The woman pressed the button for the fourth floor. The nun pressed the button for the third floor. Then the nun said, "What brings you to us, my dear?" and the woman spilled her guts. "My mother has just died, I think my father may be an alcoholic, my marriage is falling apart, and I feel like I am going crazy."

Before she could say any more, the elevator went "ding" and the doors opened. The nun gave the woman a funny little smile. "God must love you very much," she said, and disappeared through the closing doors.

"God must love you very much"? What does *that* mean?! We don't tend to think of a string of catastrophes as a sign of God's love, but that nun was clearly making some kind of connection. I am not even sure I want to know what it is, but I tell you the story because Paul seems to know about it too. In this morning's passage from his second letter to the Corinthians, he wraps up his own elevator soliloquy about the awful things that have happened to him and concludes that God must love him very much too.

The context is important. As best anyone can tell, Paul arrived in Corinth around A.D. 50. Over the next year and a half, he founded a church there. Once he was satisfied that the community was strong enough to survive without him, he set sail for Ephesus to go do the same thing all over again there. He stayed in touch with the Corinthians by mail, doing his best to instruct them long-distance, but it was not long before trouble set in. As soon as Paul left town, a new crowd of Christian evangelists arrived in Corinth—Paul calls them "super-apostles"—and began to challenge his authority. Paul was crude, they said. He was volatile and manipulative. Everywhere he went he offended people, they said (which they, presumably, did not).

Since all we have is Paul's response to their attack on him, we do not know exactly what else they said, but the gist of their argument was that Paul did not exhibit the signs of a true apostle. He was short, weak, insecure, and tactless. He did not work enough miracles. And he was always in trouble—in and out of jail, getting beaten up in public, always rubbing people the wrong way. Surely God had better taste than that, the super-apostles suggested. Surely God would tap someone more—well, more like them—to serve as true apostle, and would also offer him a smoother path.

Paul was undone by their criticism of him, especially since he knew it was true. He *was* short, weak, insecure, and tactless. He had never denied any of that, and it was as painful to him as it was to anyone else. But being an apostle had not been his idea. It was not as if he had campaigned for the job. God had forced it on him, slamming him to the ground one day and telling him what to do. God had even blinded him so he could not run away, and that was how it had been for him ever since.

By his own count, Paul had suffered five public whippings and three beatings with rods. He had been stoned once, shipwrecked three times, imprisoned more often than he could remember. When death jumped out in front of him, he hardly flinched anymore. He lived in constant danger—danger from raging rivers, danger from bandits, danger from his own people, danger from his enemies. He was used to going to bed without food or water and then lying there awake—not because he was cold and hungry, which he was, but because he was so worried about his churches.

No one was more aware than Paul of his weaknesses. He carried around a load of shame because of them, but the strange thing is that he did not try to hide them. When it came time for him to defend himself to the church in Corinth, he presented them right along with the rest of his credentials. You heard a portion of that defense a moment ago. Paul calls it his "fool's speech," because he felt like an idiot listing his virtues for his old congregation, but if boasting would win back their loyalty, then he was perfectly willing to boast.

Apparently one of the charges against him was that he was too earthy. He had plenty of experience with the church "down below," but the super-apostles suggested that any true man of

God would have more to say about what went on "up above," where only saints and angels were allowed to go. So Paul reported a vision he had had, only he was so uncomfortable bragging about it that he told it in the third person. "I know a person . . . ," he said, since he could not say "I am that person" without blushing. "I know a person in Christ who fourteen years ago was caught up in the third heaven," Paul confessed. He could not say for sure whether it was an in-the-body or out-of-the-body experience, but he knew what he saw—Paradise—and he knew what he heard there—things he was not allowed to repeat.

That did not help him very much with his credibility, since he could not go into any detail about how things were "up there," but at least Paul let his rivals know he had been there. His visit to the third heaven had elated him, Paul said, but when he came back down to earth he landed on a thorn that had been sticking him ever since. His interpretation of the thorn was that it was a messenger of Satan, a pain in the whatever that would forever after keep him from being too elated about his vision or anything else.

I do not know why that thorn has provoked so much interest through the years, but it has. Everybody wants to know what it was, but no one can say for sure. Good guesses include epilepsy, migraine headaches, malaria, depression, partial blindness, or a speech impediment. At least one person has suggested that Paul's thorn was a sexual identity he fought. Whatever it was, he could not get rid of it—and that, I think, is what fascinates us—that this holy man, who had been to the third heaven and back, who was chosen by God to be the greatest missionary of all time—this spiritual giant had something physical going on with him that bugged him every day of his life.

He was one of us, in other words. He would kneel down to say his prayers at night and feel that thing stab him. He would stand up to speak and have to wait a minute until he stopped feeling dizzy. He would try to get his mind focused on God and find himself reaching for his medicine instead. Whatever that thorn was, it got in Paul's way, so much so that he begged God not once but three times to take it away from him.

The answer to that prayer turned out to be as big a revelation for him as anything he heard in Paradise. "My grace is sufficient for you," God said, "for power is made perfect in weakness." Who would have thought it? God sits you down in front of a table with two big walnut shells on it—big enough to hide the two things God is about to show you. First God holds up a ticket to the third heaven, printed on a hummingbird feather the color of green gold. This goes under the first nutshell. Then God holds up a nasty looking thorn, brown as mud and curved like a cat's claw. This goes under the second nutshell. "Which one is the key to the power of Christ?" God says. "Keep your eye on the one you want."

Then God mixes them up, but you never take your eyes off shell number one. When God says, "Okay, choose," you are sure. You tap the shell and God says, "Right," placing the thorn in your hand.

"This game is rigged," you complain, insisting that God show you what is under the other shell. "Right again," God says, placing another thorn in your hand. "There is only one key to the power of Christ."

I suppose this can sound for all the world like divine mean-ness, but I do not believe that is what it is. Instead, I believe it is how God defends us from the super-apostles of this world, those stainless steel Christians who want to cleanse the church of prob-lematic people. Paul is our proof that God won't go along with them. God knows that being problematic is just part of being human. Every one of us suffers from some thorn or another. Every one of us has a shipwreck or two in our past, and every one of us has days—maybe even whole years—when we are short, weak, insecure, and tactless.

The good news is that none of that disqualifies us from serving God. On the contrary, those things belong on our list of credentials, because the fact that the church survives with people like us in charge is the surest proof in the world that Christ is alive and well and dwelling in us. How else could we have endured, either as individuals or as a people? God's grace is sufficient for us.

I am still not sure what that nun was trying to tell the woman in the elevator, but I think it had to do with everything that woman was about to find out—that in the very midst of her losses, with pieces of the sky still falling all around her, she was about to be more eligible than she had ever been to discover the power of Christ that is made perfect in weakness. It is the power that enables each of us, like Paul, to make our own fool's speeches, thinking back on all the awful and wonderful things that have happened to us and say, "God must love us very much."

# To Whom Can We Go?

⌐

JOSHUA 24:1−2A, 14−25
EPHESIANS 5:21−33
JOHN 6:60−69

*Because of this many of his disciples turned back and no longer went about with him. So Jesus asked the twelve, "Do you also wish to go away?" Simon Peter answered him, "Lord, to whom can we go? You have the words of eternal life. We have come to believe and know that you are the Holy One of God."*

TODAY NO ONE GETS LEFT OUT. THE APPOINTED lessons have something to offend everyone. First there is Joshua, hero of a book of wars, in which God serves as military commander of Israel's invincible army. Joshua is all cleaned up for today's speech at Shechem, but he waded through blood to get there. By divine command, he and his soldiers destroyed every major city in the promised land so that the Israelites would have room to move in. From the air, you could follow their progress by connecting the dots of smoking ruins, from Jericho to Ai to Eglon to Hebron. By God's order, Joshua and his troops wiped out the Canaanites, the Hittites, the Hivites, the Perizites, the Girgashites, the Amorites, and the Jebusites, killing every last man, woman, and child.

God helped out with the genocide at Gibeon by dumping a sky full of killer hailstones on the Amorites and by making the sun hold still in the sky so that Joshua had all the daylight he needed to make sure he had not missed anyone. The finale to this killing spree can be found in Joshua 10:40: "So Joshua defeated the whole land, the hill country and the Negeb and the lowland and the slopes, and all their kings; he left no one remaining, but utterly destroyed all that breathed, as the LORD God of Israel commanded." Is this really the Word of the Lord?

If that does not offend you, then let us move on to the letter to the Ephesians. "Wives, be subject to your husbands as you are to the Lord. For the husband is the head of the wife just as Christ is the head of the church, the body of which he is the Savior." Husbands are the saviors of their wives, in other words, and wives who disobey their husbands commit marital sin. Of course Paul also exhorts husbands to love their wives as much as they love their own bodies, and to give themselves up for their wives as willingly as Christ gave himself up for the church.

In the first century, this was fairly shocking stuff. Under Judaic law, a man's wife and children were his property. He could divorce his wife for burning his supper and he could put his daughter to death for bringing dishonor to his name. So for Paul to say that a man should treat his wife as carefully as he treated his own body was a real eyebrow-raiser for men who had been taught they could treat her however they wished. This passage was offensive then for different reasons than it is offensive now, but it was still far from a crowd pleaser.

And then there is today's gospel, the last in a four-part series on the bread of heaven. The sixth chapter of John is full of statements that were offensive to those who heard them. First Jesus suggested that he was God's own manna come down from heaven to give life to the world. We are used to hearing that sort of thing from him by now, but imagine hearing it for the first time—from a human being who does not look all that different from you—"I am the living bread that came down from heaven. Whoever eats of this bread will live forever."

Last week Jesus took the offense to an even higher level by choosing really gory words to describe what he meant. In all the other gospels, Jesus calls this bread his body. In John's gospel, he calls it his flesh—his skin and muscle tissue. In all the other gospels, he offers it to be eaten. In John's gospel he uses the word for "chomp" or "gnaw," so that a more literal translation of his invitation goes like this: "Those who chomp my flesh and guzzle my blood have eternal life; for my flesh is true food and my blood is true drink."

It is a nasty image that sounds more like something for a butcher shop than for a church. Add to that the fact that Hebrew scripture clearly forbids the drinking of blood, and you can understand why Jesus' followers began to pull away from him at that point. "This teaching is difficult," they said. "Who can accept it?"

Instead of making it easier for them to understand, Jesus made it even harder. "Does this offend you?" he said to his disciples. "Then what if you were to see the Son of Man ascending to where he was before?" *What if I were to float up into the sky right now and leave you with nothing but cricks in your necks?* He simply would not let up on them. If they were going to follow him all the way, then they were going to have to give up their need to understand, agree, or approve of everything he said or did. They were going to have to believe him, even when what he said offended them. They were going to have to trust him, even when what he did went against everything they had been taught.

You can almost hear their minds slam shut. They had hoped he was going to explain things to them so they could make reasonable decisions about how best to follow him. Instead he let them know that nothing, not even their belonging to him, was theirs to decide. "For this reason I have told you that no one can come to me unless it is granted by the Father," he said. *If you don't get it, don't blame me. God must not have chosen you.*

There must have been a terrible look on his face when he said that, a terrible sound to his voice, because plenty of his disciples turned around and left the room right then. For all we know, one or two of them spat on the floor as they did, while others simply shook their heads and walked out the door. At least twelve stayed, because according to John he asked them, "Do you also wish to go away?" He was ready for them to go. They were free to go, but Peter answered for them all. "Lord, to whom can we go? You have the words of eternal life."

Maybe it's just me, but I hear such pathos in those words. Peter is as offended as anyone else by what Jesus is saying. Of all the disciples, he is the one who stands up for traditional faith. He keeps the dietary laws. He never eats forbidden things, including any kind of meat with the blood still in it. The idea of gnawing flesh and drinking blood turns his stomach as badly as it does anyone else's, but where is he to go? As confusing as Jesus is, Peter has glimpsed something in him that he cannot turn away from. He has glimpsed God, and if trusting that means struggling with a whole lot of distasteful things that go with it, then Peter will consent to struggle. He will not give up the truth he has found, even if it comes tucked in a box full of spiders. He will not go away from the life he has been led to, even if it is miles from the life he thought he wanted.

His words have added meaning today, when so many people are wary of allying themselves with imperfect communities of faith. I hear it all the time. "If my church votes the wrong way on this issue, I am leaving." Or, "I cannot belong to a church that would fund a project like that." Or, "I don't go to church anymore.

I couldn't take any more of the 1) hypocrisy 2) sexism 3) liberals 4) conservatives 5) fundraising 6) lousy preaching 7) fill in the blank."

I believe there are good reasons to leave a church. There are probably even some good reasons to leave the church altogether, but when the main reason is that I cannot find a community of faith that agrees with me on everything from what kind of music we should sing to where we should stand on the death penalty, then I have the perfect excuse never to belong to a church with more than one member (me).

There is no perfect church, anymore than there is a perfect God, if perfect means that I understand, agree, or approve of everything that goes on. If you become a Christian, you get a Bible that says God helped Joshua exterminate whole tribes of people right down to the last baby. You get a household code that makes wives subject to their husbands and tells husbands to sacrifice themselves for their wives. You also get the parable of the prodigal son and the twenty-third psalm.

If you become an Episcopalian, you get a national church heavy with all the usual bureaucracy. You get bishops who will not ordain women and people who still want to fight about the 1928 prayer book. You also get liturgies so lovely they take your breath away, and a commitment to common prayer that puts all our divisions to shame.

Wherever people are people, there will always be things that offend. Some of them are things we should pursue until we get some agreement on them, and others we should probably leave alone—so that they can go on reminding us that there are other people in this world, just as sincere as we are, who do not see things our way. We need each other, to save us from self-righteousness. We also need each other to help keep us in shape for God. Because wherever God is God, there will always be things that offend. Like Jesus. Like fleshy bread and bloody wine. Like this church we call Christ's body, in which we are grafted to each other as surely as we are grafted to him.

Do you also wish to go away sometimes? Of course you do. We all do. But where else would we go? This is where we have heard the words of eternal life. This is where we have come to believe and know the Holy One of God. With treasures like those at hand, what offense can we not bear?

# Famine in the Land

—

AMOS 8:4–12

*The time is surely coming, says the Lord GOD, when I will send
a famine on the land; not a famine of bread, or a thirst for water,
but of hearing the words of the LORD.*

I POLLED A LOT OF PEOPLE THIS WEEK, AND THE
prophet Amos is no one's idea of a good time. "Hear this,
you that trample on the needy, and bring to ruin the poor of the
land. . . ." If you were channel-surfing on Sunday morning, would
you stick around to hear the rest of that? "On that day, says the
Lord GOD, I will make the sun go down at noon, and darken the
earth in broad daylight. I will turn your feasts into mourning, and
all your songs into lamentation; I will bring sackcloth on all loins,
and baldness on every head; I will make it like the mourning for
an only son, and the end of it like a bitter day."

Why is Amos in such a bad mood? Because the rich have
used their riches to burden those who will never work their way
out of debt. Because the clever have used their cleverness to trick
those who cannot think as fast. Because making a profit has
become more important than anything else in the land—more
important than justice, more important than sabbath, more important than God.

With stores open twenty-four hours a day, you can buy anything you want any hour of the day or night—provided you have the money to buy it with. If you do not, someone will lend it to you at twenty-five percent interest. Meanwhile, the cashier who works the graveyard shift has parked her two small children on a neighbor's couch. In the morning, before she goes home to sleep, she will transfer them to a day care center, but she is not complaining. She needs the work, even if it is part-time. If she does a good job, maybe the manager will increase her hours so she qualifies for benefits. That would take such a load off her mind—if she knew she could afford to take her kids to the doctor. What she does not know is that the manager is under strict orders to keep her hours right where they are. He may hire as many part-time cashiers as he likes, but the company cannot afford any more full-time employees.

While she punches the keys of her cash register, someone else is tapping at the keys of a computer across town. It may be nighttime on this side of the world, but it is always daytime somewhere else—someplace where banks are open and money can be moved around, even if it means the unfortunate collapse of some small government in Malaysia. That sort of thing cannot be helped. It is one of the risks you take when you sit down at the poker table of the world economy.

As the sun comes up and this gambler goes to bed, a seasoned CEO knots his tie in front of the mirror. Today is the day he meets with the financial managers of the company he has just bought. First they will go over the figures together and then he will announce what should be obvious to everyone: he cannot afford two payrolls. He is very sorry about this downside to the merger. He is especially sorry for those who were so close to retirement, but it is his business to stay in business. All employees should prepare for the transition, which will take place in thirty days. He assures everyone of his best wishes, which he will back up with letters of reference for anyone who requests them. He wants to thank those present for their time and their attention. And now, if they will excuse him, he has another meeting to attend.

"The LORD has sworn by the pride of Jacob: Surely I will never forget any of their deeds."

Amos is in a bad mood because the health of the market has become a higher good than the health of the people, and God cannot stand it anymore. It is time to expose the sickness of this system. It is time to smash the economic idol and have a proper funeral for it, with sackcloth and ashes for all the next of kin.

Most of us are used to hearing passages like this one as personal indictments, which makes them strangely easy to ignore. When the finger is jabbing you in your own chest, it is pretty easy to defend yourself. As a prophet, Amos's scope is wider than that. He is jabbing an entire nation on God's behalf. He wants to know when they all agreed things have to stay the way they are, and why they think it is all right to keep profiting from an economy that is repugnant to God.

The place was Israel and the time was twenty-seven hundred years ago, but see if parts of it do not sound familiar to you. The nation has enjoyed forty years of peace and prosperity, largely because the evil empire of Assyria has been busy with troubles of its own. Without any hot or cold wars to fight, the nation has used the lull in hostilities to grow strong. With no one watching, Israel has reclaimed lost territories and handed them over to royal friends. As the rich have gotten richer, the poor have become poorer. Some people have winter houses and summer houses, while other people have no houses at all. Some people eat medallions of veal with mushroom sauce and sip Merlot, while other people make pancakes out of wheat sweepings off the floor. The worst part is the alienation between the two. They have forgotten they are kin, and the imbalance between them has tipped the scales of justice right over.

Meanwhile, the nation's wealth and military power are being read as signs of God's favor. Religion flourishes among the prosperous, who pour money into their sacred rituals. There is a lot of talk in big houses about "thanking God for our blessings" and "welcoming the day of the Lord," when the rude fact is that a large percentage of the population is still living in hell.

This last part apparently bothers God the most. It falls under the category of taking the Lord's name in vain, so God recruits a herdsman named Amos to go challenge the theology of the upper classes. Amos does not have the education to use big words. He calls the rich men robbers and the rich women cows. He mocks their religious assemblies and condemns their offerings as failed attempts at divine bribery. He ticks off the different ways God has tried to get their attention. *I have tried famine, drought, blight, and locusts,* God says. *I have tried illness, sudden death, and political upheaval.* But none of it has worked. The nation's business is to stay in business, and it has managed to do just that.

That is when God delivers the end-of-the-world scenario we heard a little while ago, about making the sun go down at noon and darkening the earth in broad daylight. Neither of those is the scariest part, however. The scariest part is God's promise that people who ignore God's word will eventually find themselves without it. One day they will wake up to discover that God has packed up all the good words and left the country with them.

They will hunt in vain for any sign of those words. When they want to say something to heal the rifts between them, they will stand there and look at each other with blank faces. When they take their children in their arms and try to remember the word for what they feel inside of them when they do that, nothing will occur to them. When they are falsely accused, or charged twice what they owe, they will rack their brains for the word that means that is not right, but they will not be able to find it.

They will not be able to find any of the words God used to bring the world into being, such as "light," "good," or "blessing." With those words subtracted from it, the world will seem no more than a shadow of itself. The only words left will be words that drag it back down toward chaos again, words such as "darkness," "evil," "curse." When that happens, God says, people will know what a famine really is—"not a famine of bread, or a thirst for water, but of hearing the words of the LORD."

I will let you decide whether or not that prophecy has come true. Is anyone here hungry for the words of the Lord? Not religious rhetoric, not politics wrapped up in scripture, not this group declaring moral superiority over that group, but words that seem to come from beyond those who speak them, words that startle the ear with their clarity, their freshness, their power. Has anyone here run to and fro seeking such words and failed to find them?

They are rare, that is for sure. Most of us do not have the words to talk about what is important to us anymore. Plus, our ears have been so assaulted by the impostors of God that many of us are hard of hearing. Most of what we hear sounds like noisy gongs or clanging cymbals. And yet, every now and then, divine words do break through—clear notes emerging from a background of static. Sometimes they come straight out of the Bible. Other times they come through human speech, and not always in a church. I have heard God speak on the steps of the Lincoln Memorial and in a night shelter in Atlanta. I have heard God speak through jailbirds and heads of state.

The question is, how do you know? With so many words coming at you, how do you know which ones are God's and which ones are not? I am not sure there is only one answer to that question, but I am aware of things I listen out for when I am trying to tell the difference. The first thing I listen out for is arrogance. In my experience, God's subject matter is rarely surprising. God seems to stick to three or four basic themes: uncompromising love, perfect obedience, endless forgiveness, justice for all. Since any human being who speaks of such things speaks as someone who has failed to do them, enormous humility is required to pronounce these words. They almost never serve to support our own positions. They almost always yank our supports out from under us, so that we learn never to rely on our own constructs. This is not divine meanness. This is divine passion, that will not allow anything to stand between us and God—not even our own beliefs about God.

So I generally do not listen to people who quote God to support their own positions. I am also wary of people who want to coerce me, since God does not do that. The choices may be as clear as life and death. The consequences may be spelled out one-two-three, but God never takes away our freedom to choose.

The last thing I listen out for is fear. While I am extremely vulnerable to scare tactics, I try not to succumb to them. The words of the Lord may sometimes frighten, but fear is never their goal. Their goal is the healing of the cosmos. Their goal is abundant life.

Imagine a parent watching a two-year-old pick up a rattlesnake. What does the parent say? *"Drop the snake!!"* What scares us is the loud voice God sometimes uses to warn us away from things that can kill us, but it is a rare prophet who does not wind up his prophecy with a vision of homecoming. Even Amos's mood improves at the end.

"I will restore the fortunes of my people Israel," God says through him. "I will plant them upon their land, and they shall never again be plucked up."

I guess the best way to combat the famine of hearing the words of the Lord is to speak them ourselves—never with arrogance, never to coerce or frighten, always with the understanding that they are like nitroglycerine in our mouths—but also with the willingness to speak them, and better yet, to live them, as our way of letting God know we have heard the words of life.

It is not anything we are supposed to do all by ourselves. God does not call many of us to stand alone, like Amos, warning a whole nation about the snakes it picks up. What God does instead is to call us together, into communities like this one, where the words of the Lord can go to work on us, and through us, until the sound of them becomes like a heartbeat in our ears. The thing is, to let them give us life. The thing is, to let them turn our lives into blessings on all other lives, so that new crops of God's sustaining word spring up on the earth.

# The Yes and No Brothers

$\smile$

MATTHEW 21:28–32

*A man had two sons; he went to the first and said, "Son, go and work in the vineyard today." He answered, "I will not"; but later he changed his mind and went. The father went to the second and said the same; and he answered, "I go, sir"; but he did not go. Which of the two did the will of his father?*

IF THERE HAD BEEN AN INQUEST INTO JESUS' DEATH, the parable of the two brothers would probably have been presented as one of the things that got him killed. According to Matthew, Jesus told it during the last week of his life in Jerusalem—after he had stolen a donkey to ride into town on, after he had chased the merchants out of the temple, after he had cursed the fig tree for failing to bear fruit—he went back to the temple to teach, and that is where the chief priests and the elders cornered him. The main thing they wanted to know was who had given him the authority to do all those things. Who, they wanted to know, did he think he was?

Instead of answering them, he did something that was very typical for him. He asked them a question—"What do you think?"—and he told them a story. It took a little longer than giving them a straight answer, but Jesus was never one to give people answers they could come up with on their own. He knew truth is something people have to discover for themselves, so he went to the extra trouble of helping them do that, even when he knew it might backfire on him.

The story he told the chief priests and elders that day was the story of the Yes and No brothers, or at least we will call them brothers. In Matthew's Greek, they are simply two children, old enough to work in the family vineyard but still working out their relationship with their father. When he asked each of them in turn to go work in the vineyard, the No brother said he would not go but later changed his mind and went. The Yes brother said he would go but never did. Which brother, Jesus asked his critics, did the will of his father?

It was an easy answer, as easy for them as it is for us. The first brother did the will of his father, of course. It was not what either boy said that mattered but what he finally did. Only that was not the part of the truth that got Jesus killed. What got him killed was the second part, when he told the chief priests and elders which brother they were. They were the Yes men, he told them, who said all the right things, believed all the right things, stood for all the right things, but who would not do the right things God asked them to do.

They *thought* they were doing the right things, mind you, but they had gotten so attached to their own ideas about what those things were that it was hard for them to accept much correction. First John the Baptist and then Jesus suggested that they trade in their beliefs for a fresh experience of God, but they could not bring themselves to do that. They said yes to God while they acted out a great big NO to Jesus, who suggested that they might be in for a big surprise.

People they despised were going into the kingdom ahead of them, he told them—not instead of them, but ahead of them—

people who may have said no at the beginning but who changed their minds and went, while those who refused to go continued to mistake their own convictions for obedience to God.

On the one hand, it is just one more story about hypocrisy, which has always been the number one charge leveled against religious people—that we say one thing and do another, promising we will love each other on Sunday and finding a dozen ways to slander, cheat, or just plain ignore each other on Monday. It is a serious charge against those who pretend goodness, wearing a fake fur of faith in God in order to gain advantage over other people. But I do not think conscious pretense is the real problem. I am much more concerned about the unconscious way many of us substitute our beliefs about God for our obedience to God, as if it were enough to say "I go, sir," without ever tensing a muscle to get out of our chairs.

I do not know how it starts. Maybe we have such good imaginations that we actually believe we have done things we have really only thought about doing. Never mind God for a minute. Consider everyday life. Have you ever thought about visiting a sick friend, rehearsed what you wanted to say, decided on a card instead, thought about what a nice gesture that would be, congratulated yourself on your thoughtfulness, and let it go at that? I hope I am not the only one here who has done that. I have even had a hard time later remembering whether I ever sent the card or not. I believe in doing things like that. I even believe I am the kind of person who does things like that, but sometimes I do not do them. I just roll the ideas around in my mind until I have sucked all the sweetness out of them and then I swallow them.

It is easy to get beliefs mixed up with actions. Right now I know five or ten people who believe they love their families but who spend very little time with them. I know another twenty who believe in protecting the environment but who drive cars that get less than ten miles to the gallon. I know about a hundred people who believe they are against violence in movies but who stand in line for the next *Die Hard* sequel, and I even know a few people who believe in the American way but who are not registered to vote.

It is a very peculiar thing, this vacuum between what we believe and what we actually do. The theological word for it is sin—missing the mark—which is both inevitable and forgivable but never tolerable for those who love God. When God is the mark we are missing, the vacuum is simply too painful to bear. It tears us up to say one thing and do another. It tears up our families, our friendships, our communities—when we say love and do indifference, or say right and do wrong, or say "I will go" and go nowhere at all. What we believe has no meaning apart from what we do about it. There is not a creed or a mission statement in the world that is worth one visit to a sick friend, or one cup of water held out to someone who is longing for it.

Maybe you have read Isak Dinesen's wonderful book *Out of Africa*. In it, she tells the story of a young Kikuyu boy named Kitau who appeared at her door in Nairobi one day to ask if he might work for her. She said yes and he turned out to be a fine servant, but after just three months he came to her again to ask her for a letter of recommendation to Sheik Ali bin Salim, a Muslim in Mombasa. Upset at the thought of losing him, she offered to raise Kitau's pay, but he was firm about leaving.

He had decided he would become either a Christian or a Muslim, he explained, and his whole purpose in coming to live with her had been to see the ways and habits of Christians up close. Next he would go live for three months with Sheik Ali to see how Muslims behaved and then he would make up his mind. Aghast, Dinesen wrote, "I believe that even an Archbishop, when he had had these facts laid before him, would have said, or at least thought, as I said, 'Good God, Kitau, you might have told me that when you came here.'"

God does not tell us ahead of time. Or, more to the point, God has been telling us all along—that there is no shortage of people who say, believe, or stand for all the right things. There have always been plenty of those in the world. What God is short of are people who will go where God calls them and do what God gives them to do—even, say, when it goes *against* their beliefs. To quote Søren Kierkegaard, Jesus wants followers, not admirers. Whether we say yes or no to him is apparently less important to him than what we actually do. The important thing is what our lives say, and they are as easy for most people to read as the story of the Yes and No brothers. To tell which one you are, look in any mirror. What is moving? Your mouth or your feet?

# Wedding Dress

⟶

MATTHEW 22:1–14

*Then the king said to his slaves, "The wedding is ready, but those invited were not worthy. Go therefore into the main streets, and invite everyone you find to the wedding banquet." Those slaves went out into the streets and gathered all whom they found, both good and bad; so the wedding hall was filled with guests.*

O**N THE CONTINUUM BETWEEN CHURCHES WHERE** people dress up and churches where people dress down, this is definitely what you would call a "casual dress" congregation. One mother even told me that is why she comes here—because she does not have to wrestle her daughter into a dress on Sunday morning. In the summertime, people show up at the early service in shorts, the acolytes wear running shoes, and most women do not try to walk across the gravel parking lot in high heels more than once.

We dress comfortably here, which may be why we react so strongly to this morning's story about the underdressed guest. What did the king expect?! If you are going to go out into the streets and recruit guests at the last minute, how can you expect them to be wearing the right clothes? With all due respect, your highness, either give them time to go home and change or lower your standards. No one walks around in wedding robes, just in case they happen to be invited to a royal banquet.

Some scholars say that wedding hosts provided garments for their guests in those days, the same way some fancy restaurants keep a spare jacket and tie on hand for dinner guests who show up in shirt sleeves. If that was the case, then the spotlight shifts from the king to the guest. Why did he refuse the robe that was offered him? What made him think he could come as he was to such an auspicious feast without being noticed?

Either way, this is no ordinary story. It is an elaborate allegory, in which everything has a deeper meaning. Our first clue is the opening line. "The kingdom of heaven may be compared to a king who gave a wedding banquet for his son." Gee, who do you think that Son could be? Our second clue is the outrageousness of the plot. How many people do you know who murder the postal worker for delivering a wedding invitation? And how likely is it that a wedding banquet would stay warm while a king mobilized his troops, declared war, and burned a whole city to the ground? By the time all that had happened, the veal roast would be seriously overdone.

There is no way to handle this story without knowing the story behind it, which was Jesus' disappointment, and Matthew's after him, that so few of God's people were responding to the invitation to celebrate with God's son. The prophets had invited them, but some of them had killed the prophets. Then, in A. D. 70, Jerusalem was sacked by Rome. The temple was demolished right down to its retaining walls, which some interpreted as fire from heaven. Then, largely through the efforts of Saint Paul, the Jewish community of Christ's followers was opened to Gentiles—the second shift of invited guests—and new controversy set in.

The latecomers—the Gentiles who had no history with the

God of Israel—acted as if grace gave them permission to live any way they wanted to. Meanwhile, the old-timers—the Hebrews who had known God forever—were still trying to figure out what it meant for them to be free from the Law. Pretty soon, the early church had a discipline problem on its hands, as believers bellied up to God's table with no sense of what it meant for them to be there. As far as they were concerned, you showed up in God's presence however you wanted to show up, because Jesus had squared everything with God forever. The invitation to the heavenly banquet was "come as you are." All were welcome and nothing was required: no fancy clothes, no etiquette, no *RSVP.*

"Wrong," Matthew said to his congregation with this story. Being an invited guest does not mean you may do as you please. Being invited at the last minute does not mean anything goes. People of God! You have been invited to feast with the king! Rise to the occasion!

The underdressed wedding guest got bounced because he would not do that. Maybe he thought the king was lucky he came at all. Maybe he thought he was doing his host a favor by showing up to eat food that might otherwise have gone to waste, in which case he was seriously mistaken about who was doing a favor for whom. Whatever his logic, he did not rise to the occasion. Instead, he demeaned it, by refusing to change. I am not talking about clothes, either.

Like everything else in this story, the wedding robe has a deeper meaning. It is not a white linen tunic embroidered with gold thread. It is a whole way of life—one that honors the king, one that recognizes the privilege of being called into his presence, even if the invitation arrives at the last minute. The underdressed guest's mistake was not that he showed up in shorts. It was that he showed up short on righteousness and thought no one would notice, least of all the king.

On the one hand, then, this is a story that addressed a very particular situation in the life of the early church and no longer has anything to do with us. On the other hand, it happens every Sunday right here. This may not be the heavenly wedding banquet, but it is certainly the rehearsal dinner, where each of us gets a chance to practice our parts. Everyone in Habersham County was invited to be here this morning, but as you can see, some of them had other things to do. Some are on the golf course and some are at work. Some are still in bed, but we are here and not necessarily because we are better than they are. When the king's slaves went out to recruit the second batch of guests, remember, they "gathered all whom they found, both good and bad." It just so happens that for our own good and bad reasons, this is the invitation we decided to accept this morning.

But like the underdressed guest, some of us have rolled in here without thinking much about it. We have showed up with our spiritual shirttails hanging out, lining up at the buffet table as if no one could see the ways in which we too have refused to change—refusing to surrender our fears and resentments, refusing to share our wealth, refusing to respect the dignity of every human being. These are the old clothes we wear to the king's banquet—the clothes we prefer to the wedding robe of new life—and they are as painful to him as a bride dressed in black.

The truth is, some of us did not think it mattered. In most parts of the world, there are so few people in church these days that social scientists call this the post-Christian era. Most churches are happy for anyone they can get, and some of them spend small fortunes on advertising campaigns. Like the king's slaves, they are out beating the bushes for anyone they can find to fill the wedding hall, so no wonder some of us got the idea that showing up was all that mattered.

That is what the underdressed guest thought, anyway. He

thought the king was just looking for warm bodies, and he was happy to oblige. He was happy to eat the king's food and enjoy the king's music, if that would help the king out. That was just what he was doing, too—standing near the orchestra in his striped shirt and plaid pants, tapping his foot and popping one more canape into his mouth when the king walked right up to him.

"Friend," he said, saying it the way a policeman says it just before he asks you if you know how fast you were going. "Friend, how did you get in here without a wedding robe?"

God is not looking for warm bodies. God is looking for wedding guests, who will rise to the occasion of honoring the son. We can do that in shorts and running shoes, I think, as well as we can do it in suits and high heels, because our wedding robes are not made out of denim or silk. They are made from the whole fabric of our lives, using patterns God has given us—patterns of justice, forgiveness, loving-kindness, peace. When we stitch them up and put them on we are gorgeous, absolutely gorgeous. I don't know why we would want to wear anything else, especially if we want to be ready for a wedding whenever the invitation comes.

# Bothering God

LUKE 18:1–8

*And the Lord said, "Listen to what the unjust judge says. And will not God grant justice to his chosen ones who cry to him day and night? Will he delay long in helping them? I tell you, he will quickly grant justice to them."*

A T FIRST READING, JESUS' STORY ABOUT THE PER-sistent widow and the unjust judge is one of the funniest in the Christian canon. The humor dissipates, however, with his suggestion that it is a story about prayer. Apparently we too are supposed to make pests of ourselves, in hopes God will respond to us if only to shut us up.

In Luke's gospel the parable follows right on the heels of Jesus' very scary story about the end of the age. "I tell you," he says to his disciples, "on that night there will be two in one bed; one will be taken and the other left. There will be two women grinding meal together; one will be taken and the other left." Then his disciples ask him, "Where, Lord?" And he says to them, "Where the corpse is, there the vultures will gather."

Then he takes a breath and continues with the parable of the unjust judge, which is our clue that he is not talking about just any old kind of prayer. He is talking about prayer that asks

God to come and come soon—prayer that is more than a little spooked by the idea of being snatched out of bed in the middle of the night—prayer that begs for God's presence, God's justice, God's compassion—not later but right now.

As some of you know, prayer like that can wear your heart right out, if you're not careful—especially when there is no sign on earth that God has heard, much less answered, your prayer. You can only knock so long at a closed door before your hands hurt too much to go on. You can only listen to yourself speak into the silence so long before you start to wonder if anyone was ever there. When that happens—when the pain and the doubt gang up on you to the point that you start feeling dead inside—then it is time to get some help, because you are "losing heart." That is the phrase Jesus uses, and he does not want it happening to anyone he loves. That is why he told his disciples a parable about their need to pray always and not to lose heart.

I have a seven-year-old granddaughter by marriage named Madeline. She is blond, skinny, and tall for her age. When she comes to visit, we cook together. Our most successful dishes to date have been mashed sweet potatoes with lots of butter and crescent dinner rolls made from scratch. From the day Madeline was born, we have been able to look each other straight in the eye with no sentimentality whatsoever. The tartness of our love for one another continues to surprise me. It is easy to forget she is seven years old.

When she came to celebrate her birthday last summer, there were just four of us at the table: Madeline, her mother, her grandfather, and me. She watched the candles on her cake burn down while we sang her the birthday song and then she leaned over to blow them out without making a wish.

"Aren't you going to make a wish?" her mother asked.

"You have to make a wish," her grandfather said. Madeline looked as if someone had just run over her cat.

"I don't know why I keep doing this," she said to no one in particular.

"Doing what?" I asked.

"This wishing thing," she said, looking at the empty chair at the table. "Last year I wished my best friend wouldn't move away but she did. This year I want to wish that my mommy and daddy will get back together. . . ."

"That's not going to happen," her mother said, "so don't waste your wish on that."

"I know it's not going to happen," Madeline said, "so why do I keep doing this?"

Since the issue was wishing, not praying, I left her alone that afternoon, but I know that sooner or later Madeline and I are going to have to talk about prayer. I do not want that child to lose heart. I want her to believe in a God who loves her and listens to her, but in that case I will need some explanation for why it does not always seem that way.

This is the same problem Jesus was having with his loved ones. Things were not going well in the prayer department. The disciples wanted God to make clear to everyone that Jesus was who they thought he was, but instead there were warrants out for his arrest and even he was telling them that his place at the table would soon be empty. By the time Luke wrote it all down twenty years later, things had gotten even worse. Rome was standing over Jerusalem like a vulture over a corpse and there was no sign of the kingdom coming any time soon. Jesus had said he would be right back, only he was not back. People were losing heart, so Luke repeated the story that Jesus had told, about the wronged widow who would not stop pleading her case.

Luke does not say what her complaint is about, but it is not hard to guess. Since she is a widow, her case probably concerns her dead husband's estate. Under Jewish law she cannot inherit it—it goes straight to her sons or her brothers-in-law—but she is allowed to live off of it, unless someone is trying to cheat her out of it. The fact that she is standing alone in the street is a pretty good indicator that none of the men in her family is on her side. If she had any protectors left, they would have kept her home and gone about things in a more civilized manner. No son wants his mother hanging the family laundry in the street. No brother-in-law wants his brother's widow disgracing the family name.

But she has no one holding her back, and as the judge soon finds out, she is quite capable of taking care of herself. This is not a respectable judge, remember. By his own admission, he has no fear of God or respect for anyone. Maybe he thinks that makes him a better judge—more impartial and all that—or maybe he has sat on the bench long enough to know how complicated justice really is. However it happened, he is very well-defended. God does not get to him and people do not get to him, but this widow gets to him, at least partially because she throws a mean right punch.

We cannot hear the humor in the English translation, but in Luke's Greek version, the judge uses a boxing term for the widow. "Though I have no fear of God and no respect for anyone," he says, "yet because this widow keeps bothering me, I will grant her justice, so that she may not wear me out with *continued blows under the eye.*" His motivation in responding to her is not equity but conceit. He does not want to walk around town with a black eye and have to make up stories about how he got it. Anyone who has seen the widow nipping at him like a mad dog will know where he got it. Since he cannot stand that idea, he grants her justice to save face.

"Listen to what the unjust judge says," Jesus says to his disciples. This is the part he wants us to pay attention to. *Won't God do the same for you? If you too cry out both day and night, will God delay long in helping you too?*

I am trying to decide whether I really want to tell Madeline this story. What if she concludes that the way to get what she wants is to keep punching God under the eye? Worse yet, what if she gathers that God will answer her not in order to draw her closer but in order to get rid of her?

Actually, I don't think I will say much about God at all. I think I will focus on the woman instead—about how, when she found herself all alone without anyone to help her, she did not lose heart. She knew what she wanted and she knew who could give it to her. Whether he gave it or not was beyond her control, but that did not matter to her. She was willing to say what she wanted—out loud, day and night, over and over—whether she got it or not, because saying it was how she remembered who she was. It was how she remembered the shape of her heart, and while there may have been plenty of people who were embarrassed by her or felt sorry for her for exposing herself like that, there were days when she wanted to say, "Don't knock it until you have tried it!"

She would never have believed it herself—how exhilarating it was to stop trying to phrase things the right way, to stop going through proper channels and acting grateful for whatever scraps life dropped on her plate. There were no words for the relief she felt when she finally threw off her shame, her caution, her self-control and went straight to the source to say exactly what she wanted. She did not know she could roar until she heard herself do it.

*Give me justice!* she yelled at the judge. *Do your job! Answer me now or answer me later, but I am coming back every day and every night—forever—until you deal with me.*

So he dealt with her, but I am not even sure that is the point. I keep coming back to that sad little question at the end of the parable: "And yet, when the Son of Man comes, will he find faith on earth?" It makes you think that Jesus did not know too many persistent widows, or at least not enough of them. He did not know too many people with the faith to stay at anything *forever*. Then as now, most people prayed like they brushed their teeth—once in the morning and once at night, as part of their spiritual hygiene program.

Even the ones who invested more of themselves than that tended to be easily discouraged. They would hang in there for a while, maybe praying as much as an hour a day for weeks on end, but when those prayers seemed to go unanswered they would back off—a little or a lot—either by deciding not to ask so much or by deciding not to ask at all. Superficial prayers turned out to be less painful than prayers from the heart, and no prayers turned out to be the least hurtful of all. Don't ask and you won't be disappointed. Don't seek and you won't miss what you don't find. As for that growing deadness you feel where your heart used to be, well, you will just have to get used to that.

What the persistent widow knows is that the most important time to pray is when your prayers seem meaningless. If you don't go throw a few punches at the judge, what are you going to do? Take to your bed with a box of Kleenex? Forget about justice altogether? No. Day by day by day, you are going to get up, wash your face, and go ask for what you want. You are going to trust the process, regardless of what comes of it, because the process itself gives you life. The process keeps you engaged with what matters most to you, so you do not lose heart.

One day, when Madeline asks me outright whether prayer really works, I am going to say, "Oh, sweetie, of course it does. It keeps our hearts chasing after God's heart. It's how we bother God, and it's how God bothers us back. There's nothing that works any better than that."

# God of the Living

*Jesus said to the Sadducees, "Those who belong to this age marry and are given in marriage; but those who are considered worthy of a place in that age and in the resurrection from the dead neither marry nor are given in marriage. Indeed, they cannot die anymore, because they are like angels and are children of God, being children of the resurrection."*

THE SADDUCEES DO NOT REALLY WANT TO KNOW what Jesus thinks about the hypothetical woman with seven husbands. They are just trying to highlight the ridiculousness of resurrection—which, if it were true—would cause a whole lot more problems than it solved. But while their question is not sincere, Jesus' answer is. Except for a few passing references to the afterlife elsewhere in his sayings, this passage from Luke's gospel contains the sum total of Jesus' teaching on resurrection.

It is interesting that the question occurs in the context of marriage, since that is still where it tends to show up. I remember a groom who wanted to change the wedding vows in the prayer book. "Why does it say, 'until we are parted by death'?" he asked. "Why is death the end of this marriage, if we both believe in eternal life?" Good question.

But I also remember a woman who was already dying of cancer when her husband suddenly dropped dead of a heart attack. At his funeral, people leaned over her wheelchair to console her by reminding her that it would not be long until she and her husband were together again. Later, when we were alone, she looked at me with tears streaming down her face. "I am never going to get away from him, am I?" she said.

If the world to come is just a continuation of this one, then the prospect of eternal life is not something everyone looks forward to. Plus, as the Sadducees suggest, it could get really, really complicated. Their question about the woman with seven husbands is based on Jewish law, which cares less about her marriages than about her offspring. Long before the idea of resurrection ever occurred to anyone, the Israelites believed they lived on in their children. As long as there was someone to remember them—as long as there were descendants to carry on the family name as well as the family gene pool—then they still had life, even though they were long gone.

By the same token, a man who died without an heir was finished. Everything he had been and done would vanish without a trace. This was not merely a personal loss, either. It was a loss for the whole people of Israel. So God gave Moses a law by which a dead man's brother should marry his brother's widow, adding her to his own wives in hopes of producing an heir. If the couple had a son, then the boy was raised as his biological father's nephew. Legally and socially, he was the son of his mother's first husband, all set to inherit his property and keep his name alive.

It was a compassionate law, all in all, which the Sadducees made ridiculous by multiplying it times seven and turning it into a riddle. They did not subscribe to the Pharisees' belief in resurrection, which was a later development in Judaism. Not only did Moses say nothing about it, the Sadducees insisted, but it also seemed a little too—well, too human—more wishful thinking than anything solid enough to bet your life on.

I guess there is a little Sadducee in all of us. However much we want to believe, bodily resurrection does not square with the law of Moses or any other law we know about. If it is true, then it breaks all the rules, and it definitely leads to absurd situations. For instance, if resurrection is real, then what about cremation? I do not want to spend eternity in an urn. And what about people who have lost their limbs, their gall bladders, or their minds? Will they be raised with or without their missing parts? Will my old springer spaniel Chip be there or is resurrection for human beings only? Will any of us recognize each other or will we all be morphed into creatures of light?

The Bible does not answer any of these questions. It refuses to approach resurrection as a rational kind of thing at all. Instead, it talks about resurrection as a mystical kind of thing, which is based not on our belief in God but on God's belief in us—and on God's investment in the creation, the incarnation, the essential goodness of matter, bodies, flesh. It is based on our origin in God and our ongoing union with God, which means that anyone who was ever part of God's life never stops being part of it. Even if it was just for twenty minutes on a lucky day, they belong to God forever, the God who loves bodies as much as spirits and who does not file them separately the way most of the rest of us do.

You can tie your brain into knots trying to figure it out if you want to, but I do not know anyone who ever has. Jesus said next to nothing about it. It cannot be proved or even reasoned through. Physical resurrection is one of those things like quarks or romantic love that you either go for or you don't. And even if you go for it, there isn't anything very intelligent you can say about it. Saint Paul probably did as well as anybody ever has. "Listen," he said, "I will tell you a mystery! We will not all die, but we will all be changed, in a moment, in the twinkling of an eye, at the last trumpet. For the trumpet will sound, and the dead will be raised imperishable, and we will be changed" (1 Corinthians 15:51–52). Any questions?

As far as I can tell, physical resurrection ranks right up there with virgin birth as one of the major obstacles for thinking people who are otherwise inclined to embrace the Christian faith. "If I just didn't have to say the Nicene Creed," one woman complained to me recently. "Everything else is okay, but why do we have to recite something that is so clearly part of a prescientific world view?" What I did not tell her is that at least one quantum cosmologist has written a whole book on the physics of immortality. Basing his case on the scenario of a collapsing universe, in which the force of gravity wins out over the momentum of the big bang, a perfectly respectable physicist named Frank Tipler postulates something he calls the Omega Point, occurring in the very last moments of cosmic history, when matter will transcend its own destruction by an implosion of creative power. Any questions?

Tipler has been criticized by John Polkinghorne, another physicist who is also an Anglican priest. In his book *The Faith of a Physicist*, Polkinghorne rejects Tipler's forecast but agrees with him that physical resurrection is "a perfectly coherent hope," in which our souls function along the lines of DNA, carrying the unique pattern of each one of us inside our bodies and—when we die—being used by God to recreate new bodies in any future world of God's choosing. Think Jurassic Park.

It is entirely possible that you prefer the language of the Nicene Creed to the language of quantum physics, but either way I do not think resurrection is really about us at all. I think it is about God, and to focus on our own faith or lack of faith in it may be to miss the point altogether. Resurrection is not about our own faithfulness. It is a radical claim about the faithfulness of God, who will not abandon the bodies of his beloved. That is what Jesus is getting at in his answer to the Sadducees. Never mind marriage, he says first of all. Marriage is how we preserve our own lives in this world, but in the world to come that will not be necessary anymore. We will all be wed to God—the God who is able to make children out of dust, out of dry bones, out of the bits and pieces of genuine love we are able to scrape up over a lifetime of trying—"for he is God not of the dead, but of the living, for to him all of them are alive."

This is absolutely all Jesus had to say on the subject of resurrection. You can search all four of the gospels and you will find no more teaching on it. What you *will* find is that in short order he went on to test the waters for himself. He surrendered life as we know it, and when those who loved him came to perfume his body, they could not find him anywhere. When he showed up later, he showed up with a body. He ate fish, broke bread, cooked breakfast. He also walked through locked doors and vanished while people were looking right at him. He was the same but he was different, and because he was *both*, our futures may turn out to be as astounding as his.

I am not trying to convince anyone. How could I? Resurrection cannot be supported by reason anymore than it can be supported by experience. All we have are the stories, based on the unreasonable experience of people we never knew—and the choice of whether to believe them or not. If we believe them and they turn out to be wrong, then what? We will be duped, stupid, gullible, *dead*. If, on the other hand, we do not believe them and *we* turn out to be wrong—well, what a celebration and vindication of life, however incomprehensible it turns out to be.

Any way you look at it, the choice is basically this: what would you rather be wrong about? Death? Or life?

# God's Handkerchiefs

ALL SAINTS' DAY

REVELATION 7:2–4, 9–17

*After this I looked, and there was a great multitude that no one could count, from every nation, from all tribes and peoples and languages, standing before the throne and before the Lamb, robed in white, with palm branches in their hands. They cried out in a loud voice, saying, "Salvation belongs to our God who is seated on the throne, and to the Lamb!"*

MORE THAN ANY OTHER DAY OF THE YEAR, TODAY is family reunion day for the church. The Sunday after All Saints' Day is the day for pulling out the old family photograph albums and remembering where we came from. Open one and you may find Saint Francis, standing barefoot in the snow, with birds on his shoulders and his pet wolf by his side. Or maybe you will turn to Saint Joan of Arc, who led men twice her size into battle. She preferred armor to petticoats and puzzled everyone by dressing like a man, but the voices of her critics were nothing compared to the voice of God in her head. If you keep turning pages, you may come across Saint Christopher, hiking through a swollen river with his tunic hitched up around his knees, his right hand on his staff and his left around the feet of the child he is carrying on his back.

These are some of our more famous ancestors, but if you keep looking you will find others, not as well known but no less intriguing. There is Saint Maximilian, the first conscientious objector, who was drafted by the Roman army but refused to serve. His only loyalty, he said, was to the army of God. This was a great shame and sadness to his father, a veteran, who knew that his son's decision meant death. At his beheading, Maximilian noticed the shabby clothing of his executioner and, calling to his father in the crowd, asked that his own new clothes be taken off and given to the man.

A similar story is told about Saint James the Greater, brother of Saint John, who was so full of grace on his way to his death that the guard assigned to him fell on his knees and confessed faith in his prisoner's God. James raised him up by the hand, kissed him on the cheek, and said, "Peace be with you." Then both men were executed together, but their last sweet exchange lives on in the exchange of the peace that we observe to this day: "The peace of the Lord be always with you."

When you start meeting these saints, one of the first things you notice is that they were not, well, saints. Legend has it that Saint Francis rolled naked in the snow to defend himself against his lusty thoughts and Saint Christopher was on his way to work for the devil when a mysterious hermit recruited him for God instead. Saint Mary of Egypt was a prostitute for seventeen years before she became a desert mother for the next fifty and Saint Bernard was one of the organizers of the second crusade, which collapsed into any orgy of pillage and looting. Generally speaking, the saints are not distinguished by their goodness. They are distinguished by their extravagant love of God, which shines brighter than anything else about them.

"In his holy flirtation with the world," writes Frederick Buechner, "God occasionally drops a handkerchief. These handkerchiefs are called saints." This seems to suggest that saint-making is more God's business than our own, but either way the main thing is that they do exist. There really are ordinary men and women whose love of God has led them to do extraordinary things, which means none of us can shrug our shoulders and say sainthood is beyond our reach.

Take Absalom Jones, for instance, born a house slave in Delaware in 1746. He taught himself to read from the New Testament and was eventually sold to a shopkeeper in Philadelphia. There he went to a night school run by Quakers and married another slave, whose freedom he bought with his savings. Eighteen years later he was able to do the same thing for himself and became a lay minister for black membership at Saint George's Methodist Episcopal Church in Philadelphia.

He did such a good job bringing in new people that the vestry became alarmed and voted to seat black members in the balcony. No one told Absalom Jones, and when an usher tried to pry him from his pew the following Sunday, he and the whole black membership of the church walked out the door. Seven years later his congregation was admitted to the Diocese of Pennsylvania as Saint Thomas African Episcopal Church. It grew to more than five hundred members during its first year and in 1804 Absalom Jones was ordained a priest in Christ's one, holy, catholic, and apostolic church.

Or consider Constance and her companions, a group of nuns from New England who had not been in Memphis, Tennessee, more than five years when yellow fever swept through that city for the third time in a decade. More than half the people who lived there packed up their bags and left when the sickness began, but Constance and her companions stayed put. Soothing the dying with their Yankee accents, they laid cold rags on hot foreheads and emptied bedpans full of contagion. Maybe they thought God would protect them from the virus or maybe they were not think-ing about themselves at all. If you look really hard for it, you can find the round marker with all their names on it in Elmwood Cemetery in Memphis.

It would be a mistake, however, to assume that you must be dead to be a saint. Unfortunately that is one of the requirements for canonization in the Roman Catholic Church, but the truth is that there are living saints all over the place. Think Nelson Mandela, Desmond Tutu—or Osceola McCarty of Hattiesburg, Mississippi.

Almost no one in that town knew she was a saint until about three months ago. She did not look like one. She was just a laun-dress, an old black woman who had never married, dropping out of school when she was in sixth grade to begin a lifetime of wash-ing clothes. That was the year her maiden aunt came out of the hospital, unable to walk, and moved in with her family. Twelve-year-old McCarty left school to care for her and to help her mother and grandmother with the backyard laundry business. By the time her aunt recovered a year later, McCarty thought she was too far behind to return to school. "I was too big," she says, "so I kept on working."

For the next seventy-five years that is what she did, scrubbing the dark clothes on a washboard and boiling the whites in a big black pot in her backyard before hanging them all out on the line to dry. Her day started when the sun came up and stopped when it went down, and it was not until she was eighty-seven years old that anyone knew fully who she was.

That was the year she gave $150,000—her life savings—to the University of Southern Mississippi for black scholarships. Now reporters and photographers are crawling all over her, local businesspeople have pledged to match her gift, and the young woman who was awarded the first McCarty scholarship has all but adopted her. McCarty says the one question she gets asked more than any other is why she did not spend the money on herself. "I *am* spending it on myself," she answers, smiling the slyest of smiles.

On All Saints' Day, we make the very bold claim that all these people are our relatives. In the words of one beloved hymn, "They were all of them saints of God and I mean, God helping, to be one too." We have the same blood running in our veins—Christ's blood—and the same light we see shining in them shines in us too. One of the reasons we celebrate baptism on this day is that we want the new saints to meet the old ones. We want our children and all those who are new to Christ's body to know who their ancestors are, and to understand that being a saint means first and foremost belonging to God.

Whether you give yourself an A-plus or an F-minus on that count, you cannot take it back. Once you are baptized, you belong to God and all that remains to be seen is what you will do about it. Just remember that you do not have to be famous, or perfect, or dead. You just have to be you—the one-of-a-kind, never-to-be-repeated human being whom God created you to be—to love as you are loved, to throw your arms around the world, to shine like the sun.

You do not have to do it alone, either. You have all this company—all these saints sitting right here whom you can see for yourself plus those you cannot—Francis, Joan, Christopher, Maximilian, Absalom, Constance, Nelson, Desmond, and Osceola—all of them egging you on, calling your name and shouting themselves hoarse with encouragement. Because you are part of them, and they are part of you, and all of us are knit together in the communion of saints—God's handkerchiefs—dropped on the world for the love of Christ.